셰익스피어의 도덕경
그린 월드
Green World

셰익스피어의 도덕경
그린 월드 Green World
Shakespeare's Bible of The Way and Its Virtue

발행일 2025년 9월 30일
지은이 한광석
인쇄처 도서출판 태원
24349 강원특별자치도 춘천시 서부대성로 110-2
TEL (033)255-0277 E-mail tw0277@hanmail.net

ISBN 979-11-6349-151-4 (03800)
값 15,000원
ⓒ한광석, 2025, Korea
이 책은 저작권법에 의하여 보호를 받는 저작물이므로 무단 전재와 복제를 금합니다.

셰익스피어의 도덕경
그린 월드
Green World

Shakespeare's Bible of The Way and Its Virtue

한광석

일러두기

1. 『셰익스피어의 도덕경 그린월드』는 셰익스피어의 작품에 담긴 유·불·도적인 사유를 포괄하되 노자적인 사유를 중심으로 편집하였고 노자의 『도덕경』 체계를 따랐다. 81장으로 되어 있는 『도덕경』의 각 장에 맥락을 같이하는 셰익스피어의 글을 배치하고자 하였다.

2. 이 책의 각 장이 노자의 『도덕경』의 각 장의 내용과 모두 상응하지는 않는다. 노자를 중심으로 하되 기독교와 유·불·도적인 사유가 셰익스피어의 문학적인 언어로 표현된 것을 담은 책이라는 것을 말씀 드린다.

3. 이 책의 각 장의 모든 제목과 문장들은 온전히 셰익스피어의 작품에서 발췌한 것이다. 그리고 각 장에 제시된 글은 한 작품 또는 여러 작품에서 같은 맥락의 글들을 모아서 문맥에 맞게 배열된 것이다. 다만, 필요시 문맥의 자연스러움을 위해 접속사나 이음 문구를 [ ] 표시를 하고 그 안에 넣었다. 『셰익스피어의 도덕경』이 『도덕경』처럼 경구 형식을 따르다 보니 셰익스피어 글의 일부 단어나 문구를 삭제하는 것이 문맥에 더 정합성 있다고 판단되는 경우 삭제하였다. 그러나 삭제한 것은 매우 드물다.

4. 셰익스피어에 보다 깊은 관심이 있는 분들에게 도움을 주기 위해 인용된 셰익스피어의 모든 문장의 작품 출처를 부록에 정확히 밝혀 놓았다. 부록에서 셰익스

피어 영어 원문 중 생략한 부분은 ... 로 표시 하였고, 출전은 원문 아래 혹은 끝에 (막.장.행)으로 표기하였다. 예를 들어 (*A Midsummer Night's Dream* 5.1.7-17)는 『한여름 밤의 꿈』 5막 1장 7행에서 17행 까지를 나타낸다.

5. 셰익스피어 글의 영어 원문 텍스트는 실번 바닛(Sylvan Barnet)이 편집한 *The Complete Signet Classic Shakespeare* (New York: Harcourt, 1972)를 저본으로 하고 필요시 블레이크모어 에반스(Blakemore Evans)가 편집한 *The Riverside Shakespeare* (New York: Houghton, 1977)를 참고 하였다.

6. 번역문은 여러 번역판을 참고하였으나 정음사에서 1980년에 발간한 『셰익스피어 全集』(1-4권)과 김재남 선생께서 작품 전체를 번역하여 출간한 『셰익스피어 全集』(을지서적, 1995)을 가장 많이 참고 하였다.

차례

셰익스피어의 '그린 월드Green World'로의 초대 __013

셰익스피어의 도덕경 그린 월드

제1장 말없이 사랑 하라 __020
Love, and Be Silent.

제2장 아름다움은 추함이다 __022
Fair Is Foul.

제3장 현명한 바보 __023
A Witty Fool

제4장 생명의 기운인 공기에 거처와 이름을 __024
A Local Habitation and a Name to Airy Nothing

제5장 신성한 자연 __026
Divine Nature

제6장 자연의 어머니 __028
Nature's Mother

제7장 자기 얼굴의 군주 __030
The Lord of His Face

제8장 감정의 노예가 아닌 자 __032
The Man That's Not Passion's Slave

제9장 중용적 지혜 __034
Modest Wisdom

제10장 태어남과 하늘과 땅 __036
Birth and Heaven and Earth

제11장 무의 특성 __038
The Quality of Nothing

제12장 우리 눈의 그르침 __039
The Error of Our Eye

제13장	실상의 신비 __040	
	The Mystery of Things	
제14장	말로 할 수 없는 가장 희귀한 꿈 __042	
	The Rarest Dream	
제15장	존재할 것이냐, 존재하지 않을 것이냐 __044	
	To Be, or Not to Be	
제16장	무의 온전한 여정 __048	
	A Good Voyage of Nothing	
제17장	천하 만물은 스스로 그러할 뿐이다 __050	
	Ripeness Is All.	
제18장	마음속에 음악이 없는 자 __052	
	The Man That Hath No Music in Himself	
제19장	우리는 구더기를 위해 우리 자신을 살찌운다 __054	
	We Fat Ourselves for Maggots.	
제20장	학문은 성취한 만큼 잃는 것이다 __056	
	Study, - So Won, So Lost.	
제21장	일체는 희미한 대기 속으로 용해된다 __058	
	All Dissolve into Thin Air.	
제22장	자비의 본질 __060	
	The Quality of Mercy	
제23장	덕이 없으면 있는 척 하라 __062	
	Assume a Virtue, If You Have It Not.	
제24장	그대와 그대의 타고난 재능은 __064	
	Thyself and Thy Belongings	
제25장	뜨거운 얼음 __066	
	Hot Ice	
제26장	하늘을 대신하여 칼을 드는 사람은 __068	
	He Who the Sword of Heaven Will Bear	
제27장	인간이란 __069	
	Man	

제28장　시간의 자녀가 되라 __070
　　　　 Be a Child of the Time

제29장　우리의 의지와 운명 __072
　　　　 Our Wills and Fates

제30장　공정한 정의 __074
　　　　 Even-Handed Justice

제31장　모든 사람에게 공통된 이름 __076
　　　　 A Common Name to All Men

제32장　세속의 영광 __078
　　　　 Glory

제33장　나의 왕관 __079
　　　　 My Crown

제34장　인생은 한 번의 숨결 __080
　　　　 Life's but Breath.

제35장　야심을 버려라 __084
　　　　 Fling Away Ambition.

제36장　그대의 부드러움 __085
　　　　 Your Gentleness

제37장　인생은 걸어가는 그림자 __086
　　　　 Life's but a Walking Shadow.

제38장　억지로 뭘 하려는 사람들은 __088
　　　　 Willful Men

제39장　죄 없는 사람이라고 해서 __090
　　　　 Some Innocents

제40장　그 반대로 되돌아간다 __092
　　　　 The Opposite of Itself

제41장　진정한 일꾼 __094
　　　　 A True Laborer

제42장　텅 비어 널리 편재해 떠도는 대기 __096
　　　　 The Empty, Vast, and Wand'ring Air

제43장　세속에서 벗어난 숲 속의 삶 __098
　　　　Our life, Exempt from Public Haunt

제44장　명예란 무엇이냐? __100
　　　　What Is Honor?

제45장　인성의 한 가지 공통성 __102
　　　　One Touch of Nature

제46장　큰 부자 __104
　　　　Rich Enough

제47장　이 세상은 하나의 무대 __106
　　　　All the World's a Stage.

제48장　스스로 그러한대로 되게 하라 __110
　　　　Let It Be

제49장　정치는 음악처럼 __111
　　　　Government Like Music

제50장　삶의 고요한 완성 __112
　　　　Quiet Consummation

제51장　지금 이 순간 속의 미래 __115
　　　　The Future in the Instant

제52장　지옥으로 이끄는 천국 __116
　　　　The Heaven That Leads Men to Hell

제53장　하늘의 도가 공평함을 __118
　　　　The Heavens More Just

제54장　덕 있는 행위 __120
　　　　Virtuous Deeds

제55장　그대가 춤을 출 때면 __122
　　　　When You Do Dance

제56장　훌륭한 성직자 __124
　　　　A Good Divine

제57장　오만한 인간은 __126
　　　　Proud Man

제58장　슬픔이 기뻐하고, 기쁨이 슬퍼한다 __128
　　　　Grief Joys, Joy Grieves.

제59장　삶이라는 직물 __130
　　　　The Web of Our Life

제60장　아무리 미천한 곳에서라도 __132
　　　　From Lowest Place

제61장　평화의 하모니 __134
　　　　The Harmony of This Peace

제62장　악한 것에 깃든 선한 혼 __136
　　　　Soul of Goodness in Things Evil

제63장　큰 불을 __138
　　　　Mighty Fire

제64장　작은 불꽃은 __139
　　　　Small Lights

제65장　우리 자신에게 무지하니 __140
　　　　Ignorant of Ourselves

제66장　군주란 __141
　　　　Princes

제67장　가장 좋은 사람 __142
　　　　The Best Men

제68장　적에게 분노하지 마라 __144
　　　　Heat Not a Furnace for Your Foe.

제69장　장군의 장군 __145
　　　　Captain's Captain

제70장　더러운 굴껍질 속에 진주가 있듯이 __146
　　　　As Your Pearl in Your Foul Oyster

제71장　말을 삼가라 __147
　　　　Speak Less

제72장　우주의 늑대 __148
　　　　Universal Wolf

011

제73장 마음을 편히 하고 인내심을 품고 살라 __150
Bear Free and Patient Thoughts.

제74장 평온을 주는 죽음 __152
Restful Death

제75장 보잘 것 없는 이득 __154
Poor Rich Gain

제76장 맹렬한 불은 __156
Violent Fires

제77장 고결한 마음 __158
Noble Respect

제78장 덕과 지식은 __160
Virtue and Cunning

제79장 유일한 피스메이커 __162
The Only Peacemaker

제80장 새 공화국에서는 __164
In the Commonwealth

제81장 내가 주면 줄수록 __166
The More I Give to Thee

부록 Appendix:

참고한 책과 자료 __168

『셰익스피어의 도덕경 그린월드』의 셰익스피어 작품 출처 __170

셰익스피어 정전正典 목록 __212
The Shakespeare Canon

윌리엄 셰익스피어 연표 __214

셰익스피어의 '그린 월드Green World'로의 초대

　지난 여름의 더위는 그 위세가 가히 폭력적이었다. 매년 상승하는 여름의 더위가 인간의 문명이 기후변화의 심각한 위기를 초래할 만큼 '신성한 자연Divine Nature'으로 부터 너무 멀리 온 '탕자 문명'임을 실감케 한다. 문명이 브레이크가 고장 난 기관차처럼 멈출 줄 모르고 달릴수록 더위가 기승을 부릴 것이고 그에 비례해 인류의 미래는 공멸로 빠르게 다가갈 것이다. 더구나 현재 인류문명을 위협하고 실존적 위기를 초래하고 있는 것은 생태붕괴를 일으키는 기후 변화 뿐만 아니라 인공지능과 생명공학의 기술혁신에 따른 파괴의 위험까지 가세하고 있는 실정이니 우려가 클 수밖에 없다.

　문득 영화 〈설국열차〉(2013년 개봉)가 떠오른다. 인류가 지구 온난화를 해결해 보겠다고 냉각제를 살포하는 시도를 하다가 결국 빙하기를 불러일으켜 최후로 살아남은 인간들을 싣고 얼어붙은 지구 위를 끝없이 달리는 설국열차! 이제 우리가 그 열차를 타야 할 끔찍한 때가 온 듯하다. 우리가 설국열차를 타는 비극적 사태를 피하려면 이제 인류공동체 차원의 코페르니쿠스적인 사고의 전환이 필요하다.

지금까지의 서구의 기독교적인 사유와 동방의 유·불·도의 사유를 회통시켜 그 모두를 포괄하고 넘어선 진정한 인문주의에 기반한 새로운 문명을 서둘러 구축해야 한다.

영국의 평론가이자 역사가인 토마스 카알라일1795-1881은 이런 말을 한다. "셰익스피어를 인도와도 바꾸지 않겠다"고. 그의 말은 불교의 발원지인 인도 사람들이나 불교문화권의 동아시아 사람들의 입장에서 보면 매우 무례하게 들리는 발언일 수 있다. 그러나 그의 말이 함축하고 있는 의미는 불교의 인도문명이 추구하는 삶의 본질과 가치가 셰익스피어1564-1616에게도 내포되어 있다는 것이다. 우리가 셰익스피어를 접해 보면 셰익스피어에게 불교적인 사유가 짙게 깔려 있는 건 사실이다.

그런데 우리가 셰익스피어를 좀 더 가까이 들여다보면 그의 문학적 언어 세계에는 인도문명뿐만 아니라 서구의 언어 그물망에 포착되기 어려운 중국문명이 함께 공존한다. 그의 세계엔 불교의 공空사상은 물론 노자의 『도덕경』, 그리고 유가의 『중용』의 지혜가 아름다운 문학적 언어로 노래되고 있다. 셰익스피어가 살던 시대는 엘리자베스 여왕1533-1603이 대영제국을 이룩하던 르네상스 시대였다. 이 르네상스 시대는 중세 천년의 신본주의에서 벗어나 그리스·로마 고전을 부활시켜 인본주의를 꽃피우던 시대였다. 이 시대의 인본주의 정신을 구가하던 기라성 같은 작가 중에서 그 정점을 점유하고 있던 시인이자 극작가가 셰익스피어다. 유·불·도의 사상은 신을 무화시키거나 신과 거리를 두고 진작시킨 상식과 합리의 인문주의에 바탕을 두고 있어서 르네상스 인본주의 최정상급 시인이었던 셰익스피어의 사유의 맥과 크게 맞닿을 수밖에 없다.

셰익스피어는 유·불·도 중에서 특히 노자의 사유와 가장 큰 공통분모를 이룬다. 노자는 자연의 순환을 "도道"라고 하였고 그 반대로 되돌아가는 도의 순환적인 움직임으로부터 그의 사유를 풀어 간다. 자연의 순환을 토대로 하는 노자적 사유는 셰익스피어의 희극, 비극, 사극, 로맨스 극이라는 장르에 관계없이 가장 특징적으로 공유된다. 셰익스피어 극의 구조와 내용에 있어서 그의 세계를 하나로 관통하는 키 워드key word가 바로 모든 변화를 지배하는 자연법칙인 "순환"이다.

셰익스피어는 그의 성장과 활동의 문화적 배경이 기독교 문화여서 어쩔 수 없이 그의 극에는 서구적인 기독교적 사유가 편재해 있는 것은 사실이다. 그렇다 하더라도 그는 기독교의 언어를 사용하였으나 우리의 삶에 결코 신을 개입시키거나 하늘나라로의 구원을 구하지 않는다. 그는 인간의 종교적인 속박과 신화적인 비합리를 시적인 통찰과 상식적인 합리로 밀어내면서 자연의 거대한 순환적인 질서 속에서 살아가는 인간의 희노애락을 노래했을 뿐이다. 그에겐 웃고, 화내고, 슬퍼하고, 사랑하며 사는 일상의 삶 그 자체가 구원일 뿐이다. 그리고 마침내 삶을 마감하고 대지에 편안히 잠드는 것, 그것이 삶의 "고요한 완성quiet consummation"이고 전부다.

셰익스피어의 극은 대체로 '문명세계-자연세계-문명세계'의 순환 구조로 전개되고 이러한 구조는 특히 희극에서 두드러지게 나타난다. 희극은 궁정이라는 문명세계에서 분규와 갈등이 시작하여 숲이라는 자연세계로 이동하여 희극적 해결을 이룬 뒤 다시 궁정인 문명세계로 돌아오는 순환적인 구조를 지닌다. 이러한 구조는 문명을 자연에 합치시키거나 문명과 자연의 간격을 최대한 좁힐 때 조화롭고 건강하고 아름다운 문명이 된다는 셰익스피어의 문명관을 깊게 반영한다.

셰익스피어의 숲은 꿈과 무의식의 세계다. 그곳에선 변신 metamorphosis이 이루어지며 소망이 충족된다. 또한 인간의 인위적인 도덕이나 가치가 전도된다. 노자의 언어를 빌리면, 채움을 특징으로 하는 문명의 '실實'의 세계가 아니라 비움의 '허虛'의 세계다. 이 숲의 세계는 대립과 갈등, 음모와 찬탈로 점철되는 남성들의 궁중세계와는 달리 여성이 주도하여 이루어 내는 화해와 조화의 부드러운 세계다. 생명의 '스스로 그러함自然'이 보장되는 자유롭고 유쾌한 세계인 것이다.

셰익스피어의 이러한 숲의 자연세계를 셰익스피어 학자들은 '그린 월드Green World'라고 명명한다. 그린 월드에서는 자연과 인간이 화해되고, 모든 존재가 있는 그대로 긍정되며, 신의 세계와 인간의 세계가 분리되지 않는다. 한 마디로 그린 월드는 우리가 꿈꾸고 소망하는 세계로 우리의 불건강한 문명이 치유 받고 건강을 회복하기 위해 되돌아가야 하는 노자의 '스스로 그러한' 세계, 무한한 생명력이 잠재해 있는 '허'의 세계인 것이다. 노자와 셰익스피어의 언어는 우리 문명을 각성시켜 그린 월드로 나아가게 하는 반문명적인 건강한 기능과 역할을 한다.

셰익스피어는 희극에서는 그린 월드를 궁정세계와 대비시켜 공간적으로 떨어진 숲으로 설정한다. 그러나 사극과 비극에서는 그린 월드를 선술집의 디오니소스적인 세계나 선승 같은 깨우침의 해학과 위트를 토해내는 '현명한 바보wise fool'들을 등장시켜 문명의 생활공간 안에 설정한다. 셰익스피어는 건강하고 유쾌한 삶을 영위하기 위해선 우리의 일상생활권 안에 그린 월드를 만들어 확장시켜 가며 살아야함을 매우 강하게 권유한다. 정치란 바로 이러한 그린 월드를 확장하여 백성들이 <u>스스로 그러함</u>을 누리며 살 수 있도록 보장해야 한다는 것이다. 선불교의 관점에서 보면 셰익스피어의 37작품 전체가 하나의 공안이라고 할 수 있다. 마찬가지로 인문학적 관점에서 보면 셰익스피어 37작품 전체가 하나의 그린 월드라고 할 수 있다.

나는 이 땅의 사람들이 푸른 생명의 기운이 바다의 물결처럼 춤추는 그린 월드에서 '시간의 자녀child of time'들이 되어 살 수 있기를 소망하여 이 책을 기획하였다. 특히 '(사)셰익스피어와 함께하는 세상'에서 올해 1월에 설립한 '셰익스피어 평화학당'의 온라인 강의에 참여하는 분들 덕분에 오래 전부터 준비해온 이 책을 서둘러 완성하게 되었다. 셰익스피어를 통해 인문주의적인 새로운 사유를 창발하기 위해선 그의 37 작품을 모두 읽으면 좋겠지만, 그의 유·불·도적인 세계를 한권에 담아 함께 읽어 가는 것이 큰 도움이 되리라 생각한다. 이 책을 통해 유·불·도 를 포함하여 노자적인 사유가 셰익스피어의 문학적인 언어로 변주되는 것을 감상하는 기쁨이 있기를 소망한다.

이 책이 이 땅에 빛을 보도록 성원을 아끼지 아니하신 셰익스피어 평화학당 모든 분들께 이 자리를 빌어 큰 감사를 드린다. 그리고 바쁜 출판 일정에도 불구하고 우선적으로 이 책의 편집과 발간을 위해 공들여 주신 도서출판 태원 사진환 대표님과 박윤미 과장님께 고마움을 전한다. 끝으로 할 일을 잊고 원고와 씨름하는 나를 인내와 배려로 지원해 준 내 가족에게 깊은 감사를 드린다.

2025. 9. 1

셰익스피어의 도덕경
그린 월드 Green World

제1장 말없이 사랑 하라

말없이 사랑하라.
진실한 사랑은
말로 할 수가 없다.
진실은 아름답게 꾸미는 말보다는
행동으로 드러나는 법이다.
진리는 고요한 가슴을 지닌다.
진리를 말로 담아내지 말라.
줄리엣에게 원수인 것은
로미오 몬테규라는 이름일 뿐이다.
그는 몬테규가 아니더라도
자기 자신 그 자체다.
몬테규란 무엇인가?
그것은 손도 아니고 발도 아니며
그렇다고 팔도 아니고 얼굴도 아니며
사람 몸의 어떤 부분도 아니다.
그 어떤 다른 이름으로
불리어도 되는 것이다.
도대체 이름에 무엇이 있는가?
우리가 장미꽃에
어떤 다른 이름을 붙여도
그 향긋함을 풍기기는 마찬가지다.
그러므로

로미오는 로미오라고 불리지 않는다 하더라도
이름에 관계없이
그가 본래 지니고 있는
더할 나위 없는 온전함은
그대로 지니고 있는 것이다.

Chapter 1 Love, and Be Silent.

Love, and be silent.
[True love] cannot speak;
For truth hath better deeds than words to grace it.
Truth hath a quiet breast.
Truth should be silent.
'Tis but [the name of Romeo Montague] that is [Juliet's] enemy.
[He is himself], though not a Montague.
What's Montague? It is nor hand, nor foot,
Nor arm, nor face, nor any other part
Belonging to a man. O, be some other name.
What's in a name? That which we call a rose
By any other word would smell as sweet.
So Romeo would, were he not Romeo called,
Retain that dear perfection which he owes
Without that title.

제2장 아름다움은 추함이다

아름다움은 추함이고,
추함은 아름다움이다.
좋음과 나쁨은 없다.
단지 분별적인 생각이
그렇게 만들 뿐이다.
"예"와 "아니오" 역시
제대로 된 신학이 아니다.

Chapter 2   Fair Is foul.

Fair is foul, and foul is fair.
There is nothing either good or bad,
but thinking makes it so.
"Ay" and "no" too [is] no good divinity.

제3장 현명한 바보

어리석은 똑똑함보다는 현명한 바보가 낫다.
똑똑함 속에서 부화한 어리석음은
똑똑함의 보증과 학식의 뒷받침을 받아
고상을 떨며 유식한 바보를 포장한다.
바보들의 어리석음은 똑똑한 자들이
저지르는 우매함만큼 눈에 띄지 않는다.
바보가 현명하게 드러내는 어리석음은 잘 들어맞지만,
똑똑하다고 하는 자들이 어리석음에 빠지면
자신들의 똑똑함을 꼴불견으로 만들어 놓는다.

Chapter 3 A Witty Fool

Better a witty fool than a foolish wit.
Folly, in wisdom hatched,
Hath wisdom's warrant and the help of school
And wit's own grace to grace a learned fool.
Folly in fools bears not so strong a note
As fool'ry in the wise when wit doth dote.
Folly that [the fool] wisely shows, is fit;
But wise men, folly-fall'n, quite taint their wit.

제4장 생명의 기운인 공기에 거처와 이름을

미친 사람,
사랑에 빠진 사람,
시인은
상상력으로 꽉 차 있는 사람들이다.
한 사람은
거대한 지옥 속의 악마들보다
더 많은 악마들을 바라보니
이 사람이 미친 사람이다.
사랑에 빠진 자도
미쳐있기는 마찬가지,
집시의 얼굴에서
헬렌의 아름다움을 바라본다.
시인은
고상하게 격앙된 눈을 번득거리면서
하늘에서 지상으로,
지상에서 하늘로 훑어본다.
상상이 미지의 것에 몸의 형체를 부여하듯이,
시인의 펜은 미지의 것을 형상화하며,
보이지 않는 생명의 기운인 공기에
이름을 지어 주고 거처를 마련해 준다.

Chapter 4　A Local Habitation and a Name to Airy Nothing

The lunatic, the lover, and the poet
Are of imagination all compact.
One sees more devils than vast hell can hold,
That is the madman. The lover, all as frantic,
Sees Helen's beauty in a brow of Egypt.
The poet's eye, in a fine frenzy rolling,
Doth glance from heaven to earth, from earth to heaven;
And as imagination bodies forth
The forms of things unknown, the poet's pen
Turns them to shapes, and gives to airy nothing
A local habitation and a name.

제5장 신성한 자연

태양은
왕궁을 비추는 바로 그 얼굴을
시골 초가집에도 숨기지 아니하고
똑 같이 바라본다.
대지는
사람이나 짐승이나
다 같이 먹여 길러준다.
자연은
모든 풍작과 풍요로움을 가져와
무지무욕의 사람들을
먹여 살린다.

Chapter 5 Divine Nature

The self-same sun that shines upon his court
Hides not his visage from our cottage, but
Looks on alike.
Our dungy earth alike
Feeds beast as man.
Nature should bring forth,
Of it own kind, all foison, all abundance,
To feed my innocent people.

제6장 자연의 어머니

자연의 어머니인 대지는
자연의 무덤이기도 하고
자연이 묻히는 무덤인가 하면
자연의 자궁이기도 하다.
그리고 그 자궁에서 태어난
다양한 종류의 아이들이
대지의 따뜻한 가슴에서
젖을 빨고 있다.
여러 가지 탁월한 약효를
지닌 것이 적지 않고
어느 하나 약효를 지니지 않는 것이 없으며
그 약효는 가지각색으로 다양하다.
초목과 풀, 그리고 돌 할 것 없이
만물의 본질 속에는 놀라운 효능이 있어
아무리 흉측한 것이라 하더라도
어떤 특별한 약효를 세상에
베풀지 않는 것은 없다.
그러나 아무리 좋은 것이라고 해도
옳게 사용하지 아니하면
그 본성에 어긋나서
악용의 해를 면치 못하는 법이다.
덕 자체도 잘못 사용되면 악으로 변하고
악도 때로는 활용하기에 따라서 가치가 있게 된다.

Chapter 6 Nature's Mother

The earth that's Nature's mother is her tomb.
What is her burying grave, that is her womb.
And from her womb children of divers kind
We sucking on her natural bosom find,
Many for many virtues excellent,
None but for some, and yet all different.
O, mickle is the powerful grace that lies
In plants, herbs, stones, and their true qualities;
For naught so vile that on the earth doth live
But to the earth some special good doth give;
Nor aught so good but, strained from that fair use,
Revolts from true birth, stumbling on abuse.
Virtue itself turns vice being misapplied,
And vice sometime by action dignified.

제7장 자기 얼굴의 군주

남을 해칠만한 힘을
지니고 있으면서도
아무도 해치지 않으며
자신이 가장 으스댈 수 있는 일조차
행하지 않는 사람,
남을 감동시키면서도
자신은 돌처럼 견고하고 냉정하여
유혹에 쉽게 넘어가지 않는 사람,
이런 사람들은
하늘의 덕성을 옳게 물려받았고
자연의 재산을 낭비하지 않고
신중히 아껴 쓰는 것이다.
이들이야말로
자기 얼굴의 군주이자 주인이니
다른 사람들은
그들 탁월함의 하인들일 뿐이다.
여름 꽃은 여름을 아름답게 해준다.
비록 그 자체는 피었다 시들 뿐이지만.
그러나 이 꽃이 나쁜 병에 감염되면
가장 천한 잡초조차도
그 여름 꽃의 품위를 능가하게 된다.
가장 향기로운 것도 그들 행위에 따라

가장 더러운 냄새를 내게 된다.
썩은 백합은 잡초보다도
훨씬 더 고약한 악취를 풍긴다.

Chapter 7 The Lord of His Face

They that have pow'r to hurt and will do none,
That do not do the thing they most do show,
Who, moving others, are themselves as stone,
Unmoved, cold, and to temptation slow;
They rightly do inherit heaven's graces
And husband nature's riches from expense;
They are the lords and owners of their faces,
Others but stewards of their excellence.
The summer's flow'r is to the summer sweet,
Though to itself it only live and die;
But if that flow'r with base infection meet,
The basest weed outbraves his dignity:
For sweetest things turn sourest by their deeds;
Lilies that fester smell far worse than weeds.

제8장 감정의 노예가 아닌 자

온갖 고통을
다 겪으면서도
어느 것도
고통스러워하지 않는 사람,
운명의 시련과 보답을
똑같이 고마운 마음으로
받아들이는 그런 사람,
혈기와 분별력이
아주 잘 조화를 이루어
운명이란 여신이
제 기분에 따라
손가락을 놀리는 대로
소리 내는 피리가 아닌 사람들은
축복받은 자들이다.
감정의 노예가 아닌 사람을
내게 데려다 주면
나는 그를 내 가슴의 한복판
깊숙이 간직할 것이다.

Chapter 8 The Man That's Not Passion's Slave

One, in suff'ring all, that suffers nothing,
A man that Fortune's buffets and rewards
Hast ta'en with equal thanks; and blest are those
Whose blood and judgment are so well commeddled
That they are not a pipe for Fortune's finger
To sound what stop she please. Give me that man
That is not passion's slave, and I will wear him
In my heart's core, ay, in my heart of heart.

제9장 중용적 지혜

가장 달콤한 꿀은
그 단맛 때문에 싫어지게 되고
맛을 보고나면 입맛도 없어진다.
너무 먹을 것이 많아
포식하는 것도
먹을 것이 없어
굶주리는 것처럼 병이다.
그러므로
넘침과 모자람이 없는 것이
커다란 행복이다.
도를 지나쳐 살면
흰 머리카락이 빨리 늘어나지만
중용의 생활을 하게 되면
오래 오래 살 수 있는 것이다.
그리고 까마귀 울음소리도
곁에 아무것도 없다면
종달새 노래같이 아름답게 들린다.
그러나 소쩍새라도,
대낮에 거위 떼들이 떠드는 속에서 노래하면
굴뚝새 보다 나을 것이 없다.
모든 것은 제철을 만나야
제대로 된 찬탄을 받게 되고
완벽의 맛을 내는 법이다.

Chapter 9   Modest Wisdom

The sweetest honey
Is loathsome in his own deliciousness
And in the taste confounds the appetite.
They are as sick that surfeit with too much as they
that starve with nothing. It is not mean happiness, therefore,
to be seated in the mean; superfluity comes sooner
by white hairs, but competency lives longer.
[And] the crow doth sing as sweetly as the lark
When neither is attended; and I think
The nightingale, if she should sing by day
When every goose is cackling, would be thought
No better a musician than the wren.
How many things by season, seasoned are
To their right praise and true perfection!

제10장 태어남과 하늘과 땅

그대 인간은 태어날 때
하늘과 땅이 함께 하여
천지와 한 몸이 된 존재이다.
그러므로
인간이 이렇게 되고 저렇게 되는 것은
모두 자신에게 달려 있다.
우리의 몸은 정원이고
우리의 의지는 정원사이다.
따라서 쐐기풀을 심든, 상추를 심든,
히솝풀을 심고 백리향을 없애든,
한 가지 식물로만 기르든,
아니면 가지각색의 다양한 식물로 가꾸든,
게을러서 황무지로 만들어 놓든,
부지런히 거름을 주든,
그리 할 힘과 바로 잡을 권한은
모두 우리 의지에 놓여 있는 것이다.
마음을 즐거움과 흥겨움 쪽으로 돌려보라
그러면 수많은 해악을 물리치고
오래 오래 천수를 누리게 될 것이다.

Chapter 10 Birth and Heaven and Earth

Birth and heaven and earth, all three do meet
In thee at once. [Thus] 'tis in ourselves that we are thus,
or thus. Our bodies are our gardens, to the which our wills
are gardeners; so that if we will plant nettles or sow lettuce,
set hyssop and weed up thyme, supply it with one gender
of herbs or distract it with many - either to have it
sterile with idleness or manured with industry – why,
the power and corrigible authority of this lies in our wills.
Frame your mind to mirth and merriment,
Which bars a thousand harms and lengthens life.

제11장 무無의 특성

무無를
이롭게 쓸 줄 모르는가?
무無란
단지 드러나지 않은 것일 뿐이다.
그 무가 모든 것을 가져다준다.
나를 비롯해
인간이면 누구나 다 비워
무로 돌아가 편안해질 때까지는
그 어느 것에도
만족하지 못한다.

Chapter 11 The Quality of Nothing

Can you make no use of nothing?
Nothing is
But what is not.
Nothing brings me all things.
Nor I, nor any man that but man is,
With nothing shall be pleased, till he be eased
With being nothing.

제12장　우리 눈의 그르침

눈이 현혹되어
마음을 지배하고
현혹이 이끄는 대로 향하면
일을 그르친다.
눈에 좌우되는 마음은
타락으로 가득 차게 된다.
또한 우리의 마음은 종종
우리의 귀에 의해
더럽혀진다.

Chapter 12 The Error of our Eye

The error of our eye directs our mind.
What error leads must err.
Minds swayed by eyes are full of turpitude.
By our ears our hearts oft tainted be.

제13장 실상의 신비

위안이 생길 듯한
바로 그 샘에서
슬픔이 솟아오른다.
좋은 자궁이
나쁜 아들을 낳는다.
달콤한 사랑도
그 성질이 변하면서
가장 불쾌하고
치명적인 증오로
변해 버린다.
현재의 즐거움도
감정의 변화로 내려앉으면서
자신의 반대가 되어버린다.

Chapter 13 The Mystery of Things

From that spring whence comfort seemed to come
Discomfort swells.
Good wombs have borne bad sons.
Sweet love, changing his property,
Turns to the sourest and most deadly hate.
The present pleasure,
By revolution low'ring, does become
The opposite of itself.

제14장 말로 할 수 없는 가장 희귀한 꿈

난 참으로
희귀한 환영을 보았다.
꿈을 꾸었는데
인간의 머리로는
그게 무슨 꿈인지
말할 수 없다.
그 꿈을 설명하려 든다면
그 자는 나귀 같은 바보일 뿐이다.
누구도 그게 뭔지
말 할 수 없다.
내가 꾸었던 걸
말해 주려 한다면
인간은 얼룩 옷을 입은
바보일 뿐이다.
내 꿈이 무엇이었는지
인간의 눈으로 듣지도,
인간의 귀로 보지도,
인간의 손으로 맛볼 수도,
혀로 이해 할 수도,
마음으로 말할 수도 없다.

Chapter 14 The Rarest Dream

I have had a most rare vision. I have had a dream,
past the wit of man to say what dream it was.
Man is but an ass, if he go about to expound
this dream. Methought I was - there is no man
can tell what. Methought I was – and methought
I had – but man is but a patch'd fool, if he will offer
to say what methought I had. The eye of man hath
not heard, the ear of man hath not seen, man's hand
is not able to taste, his tongue to conceive, nor his
heart to report, what my dream was.

제15장 존재할 것이냐, 존재하지 않을 것이냐

존재할 것이냐, 존재하지 않을 것이냐,
그것이 문제로다.
난폭한 운명의 돌팔매와 화살을 맞고도
그저 꾹 참고 견디는 것이 더 고결한 정신이냐,
아니면 밀려오는 환난의 조수를 두 손으로 맞서서
끝을 내는 것이 더 고결한 정신이냐.
죽는다는 것, 그것은 잠드는 것, 단지 그뿐이다.
잠 한번으로 육신이 물려받은 가슴앓이와
수천가지 타고난 번뇌를 끝낼 수 있다면,
그것은 더 이상 바랄게 없는 삶의 완성!
죽는다는 것은 잠드는 것.
잠을 잔다! 그러면 꿈도 꾸겠지.
아! 그렇지, 여기에 걸림돌이 있구나.
우리가 이 육신의 굴레를 벗어 던지고
죽음의 잠에 빠질 때 어떤 꿈을 꾸게 될지 생각하면
그만 멈추어 설 수 밖에.
이러한 망설임 때문에 한평생 불행을 끌고 가는 것이지.
사람이 단 한 자루의 단검으로
자신의 목숨을 깨끗이 끝낼 수만 있다면
어느 누가 세상의 채찍과 조소,
폭군의 횡포, 세도가의 모욕, 버림받은 사랑의 고통,
법률의 태만, 관리들의 오만, 덕 있는 사람에게 가하는 소인배의 발길질, 이 모든 것들을 견디며 살겠는가?
나그네 한 번 가면 돌아오지 못하는 저 미지의 나라 죽음,
그 사후의 세계에 대한 두려움이 우리의 의지를 흔들어
알지 못하는 저 세계로 날아가느니
차라리 여기서 환난을 견디며 살도록 만들어 버리지 뭐냐!
그렇지 않다면 어느 누가 무거운 삶을 버겁게 걸머지고
지루한 인생길에서 신음하며 진땀을 빼겠는가?
그래서 분별심은 우리 모두를 겁쟁이로 만들고
결심의 붉은 혈색 위엔 사색의 창백한 병색이 그늘져
의기충천하던 원대한 계획도 흐름이 틀어져
실행이라는 이름조차 잃어버리고 만다.

Chapter 15 To Be, or Not To Be

To be, or not to be: that is the question:
Whether 'tis nobler in the mind to suffer
The slings and arrows of outrageous fortune,
Or to take arms against a sea of troubles,
And by opposing end them. To die, to sleep -
No more - and by a sleep to say we end
The heartache, and the thousand natural shocks
That flesh is heir to! 'Tis a consummation
Devoutly to be wished. To die, to sleep -
To sleep - perchance to dream: ay, there's the rub,
For in that sleep of death what dreams may come
When we have shuffled off this mortal coil,
Must give us pause. There's the respect
That makes calamity of so long life:
For who would bear the whips and scorns of time,
Th' oppressor's wrong, the proud man's contumely,
The pangs of despised love, the law's delay,
The insolence of office, and the spurns
That patient merit of th' unworthy takes,
When he himself might his quietus make

With a bare bodkin? Who would fardels bear,
To grunt and sweat under a weary life,
But that the dread of something after death,
The undiscovered country, from whose bourn
No traveler returns, puzzles the will,
And makes us rather bear those ills we have,
Than fly to others that we know not of?
Thus conscience does make cowards of us all,
And thus the native hue of resolution
Is sicklied o'er with the pale cast of thought,
And enterprises of great pitch and moment,
With this regard their currents turn awry,
And lose the name of action.

제16장 무의 온전한 여정

알렉산더는 죽어
땅에 묻혔다.
그는 진토로 돌아간 것이고,
진토는 흙이다.
그 흙에서 찰흙을 만드는 것이고.
그렇다면,
결국 사람들이
알렉산더 대왕이 변한
그 찰흙으로 맥주통 마개를
만들지 않았겠는가?
제왕 시저도
죽어 흙이 되었으니
바람막이 구멍에
땜질이나 되었을 것이다.
오! 천하를 두려움에
떨게 하던 그 흙덩이도
한갓 벽 땜질이 되어
한겨울의 삭풍을
막고 있을 뿐이다!

Chapter 16   A Good Voyage of Nothing

Alexander died, Alexander was buried, Alexander returneth
to dust; the dust is earth; of earth we make loam;
and why of that loam whereto he was converted might
they not stop a beer barrel?
Imperious Caesar, dead and turn'd to clay,
Might stop a hole to keep the wind away.
O, that that earth which kept the world in awe
Should patch a wall t' expel the winter's flaw!

제17장 천하 만물은 스스로 그러할 뿐이다

만물은
스스로 그러한 대로
영글어 갈 뿐이다.
그러므로
악어란 놈은
스스로 생긴 대로 생겼고,
넓이는 자기가 넓을 만큼 넓고,
키는 꼭 자신의 키 만큼 크며,
자기의 팔다리로 움직여 다닌다.
자신을 성장시켜주는 것을 먹고 살며,
일단 생명의 구성요소가
몸에서 빠져나가면 전생한다.
빛깔 역시 자기의 빛깔 그대로이다.

Chapter 17 Ripeness Is All.

Ripeness is all.
[Crocodile] is shaped, sir, like itself, and it is as broad as it hath breadth; it is just so high as it is, and moves with it own organs. It lives by that which nourisheth it, and the elements once out of it, it transmigrates. Of it own color too.

제18장 마음속에 음악이 없는 자

옛 시인은
뛰어난 시인이자 음악가인 오르페우스가
나무와 돌, 심지어 강물까지도
끌어 당겼다고 전한다.
왜냐하면
음악을 듣고 감동하여 잠시 동안이지만
그의 천성을 바꾸지 아니할 만큼
냉정하고 완고하고 광포한 자는 없으니까.
마음속에 음악이 없는 사람,
감미로운 음악에 감동되지 않는 사람,
이런 사람은 배신, 음모, 강도짓이나
하기에 딱 맞는 인간이다.
그의 정신작용은 어두운 밤처럼 우둔하고,
그의 감정은 지하세계처럼 어둡다.
그런 사람은 믿어서는 아니 된다.

Chapter 18 The Man That Hath No Music in Himself

              The poet
Did feign that Orpheus drew trees, stones, and floods;
Since naught so stockish, hard, and full of rage
But music for the time doth change his nature.
The man that hath no music in himself,
Nor is not moved with concord of sweet sounds,
Is fit for treasons, stratagems, and spoils;
The motions of his spirit are dull as night,
And his affections dark as Erebus.
Let no such man be trusted.

제19장 우리는 구더기를 위해 우리 자신을 살찌운다

당신의 구더기가
식사에는 당신의 유일한 황제이다.
우린 우리를 살찌우기 위해
모든 짐승을 살찌게 하며,
또한 우리는 구더기를 위해
우리 자신을 살찌운다.
통통한 왕이나 깡마른 거지나
다양한 식사일 뿐.
다시 말해
음식은 둘이나 한 식탁에 오른다.
어떤 사람이
왕을 잡수신 구더기로
물고기를 낚을 수 있고
그 구더기를 삼킨 물고기를
먹을 수 있다.
왕이라는 자도
거지 창자 속을 한 바퀴
행차할 수 있는 것이다.

Chapter 19 We Fat Ourselves for Maggots.

Your worm is your only emperor for diet. We fat all creatures else to fat us, and we fat ourselves for maggots. Your fat king and your lean beggar is but variable service - two dishes, but to one table.
A man may fish with the worm that hath eat of a king, and eat of the fish that hath fed of that worm.
A king may go to progress through the guts of a beggar.

제20장 학문은 성취한 만큼 잃는 것이다

학문이라는 것은
하늘에 작열하는 태양과 같다.
그것은 찡그린 얼굴을 지어본들
깊이 들여다보아지지 않는다.
꾸준히 공부하는 사람이라고 해봐야
소득이라곤 보잘 것 없어
남의 책에서 얻은
하찮은 지식의 권위 정도 말고는
별 것 없는 것이다.
하늘에 붙어있는 별들에게
이름을 붙여주는
하늘의 광체를 연구하는 천문학자나
무슨 별인지도 모르며
걸어 다니는 사람이나
반짝이는 밤하늘의 혜택을 받기는
다를 바가 없다.
학문은 언제나 빗나가기 일쑤다.
원하는 바를 얻기 위해 학문을 하는 동안
해야 할 일을 해야 함을 잊는다.
그러므로
가장 애써서 추구한 것을 얻고 보면
불을 질러 점령한 도시와 같이
그만큼 쟁취했으되 그만큼 잃은 것이다.

Chapter 20   Study, - So Won, So Lost.

Study is like the heaven's glorious sun,
That will not be deep-searched with saucy looks.
Small have continual plodders ever won
Save base authority from others' books.
These earthly godfathers of heaven's lights,
That give a name to every fixed star
Have no more profit of their shining nights
Than those that walk and wot not what they are.
Study evermore is overshot.
While it doth study to have what it would,
It doth forget to do the thing it should;
And when it hath the thing it hunteth most,
'Tis won as towns with fire - so won, so lost.

제21장 일체는 희미한 대기 속으로 용해된다

우리 삶의 축제는 끝이 난다.
그 축제의 배역을 맡은
우리 배우들은 모두 생령들이고
대기 속으로, 희미한 대기 속으로
용해되어 사라진다.
구름을 모자로 쓴 드높은 탑,
웅장한 궁전, 장엄한 신전,
이 거대한 지구 자체도,
지구상의 삼라만상 그 모두가
바탕이 없는 구성체인 환영처럼,
마침내는 용해되어
흔적조차 남기지 않는다.
우리 인간은
꿈을 이루고 있는
그런 재질로 되어 있고
우리네 짧은 인생은
한바탕의 잠으로 끝난다.

Chapter 21 All Shall Dissolve into Thin Air.

Our revels [will be] ended.
These our actors [are] all spirits and
[will be] melted into air, into thin air;
And, like the baseless fabric of this vision,
The cloud-capped towers, the gorgeous palaces,
The solemn temples, the great globe itself,
Yea, all which it inherit, shall dissolve,
And, like this insubstantial pageant faded,
Leave not a rack behind. We are such stuff
As dreams are made on, and our little life
Is rounded with a sleep.

제22장 자비의 본질

자비란
본래 강요되는 것이 아니다.
그것은 하늘에서 이 지상으로
내리는 단비와 같은 것이다.
자비는 이중의 축복을 받는다.
자비를 주는 자를 축복하며,
자비를 받는 자를 축복한다.
자비야말로
최고의 권력자가 지니는
가장 강력한 힘이다.
제왕을 제왕답게 하는 것은
그의 왕관이라기보다는
바로 이 자비심이다.
군왕이 손에 쥔 왕홀은
지상 권력의 상징이자 위엄의 표징으로
군왕에 대한 두려움과 공포를 의미할 뿐이다.
그러나 자비는 이 왕홀을 초월하여
군왕의 가슴속 옥좌에 앉아 있다.
말하자면 자비는 하느님의 속성이다.
그러므로
자비를 가지고 정의를 부드럽게 할 때
지상의 권력은 신의 권력에
가장 가까워지는 것이다.

Chapter 22 The Quality of Mercy

The quality of mercy is not strained;
It droppeth as the gentle rain from heaven
Upon the place beneath. It is twice blest;
It blesseth him that gives and him that takes.
'Tis mightiest in the mightiest; it becomes
The throned monarch better than his crown.
His scepter shows the force of temporal power,
The attribute to awe and majesty,
Wherein doth sit the dread and fear of kings;
But mercy is above this scept'red sway;
It is enthroned in the hearts of kings,
It is an attribute to God Himself,
And earthly power doth then show likest God's
When mercy seasons justice.

제23장 덕이 없으면 있는 척 하라

덕이 없으면
있는 척 시늉이라도 하라.
저 습관이란 괴물은
사악한 습성이 있어
우리의 올바른 감각을 먹어 치우지만,
한편으론 우리에게 천사도 되어준다.
그놈은
우리의 선하고 아름다운 습관적 행위엔
아주 잘 어울리는
옷과 외투를 입혀준다.
오늘 하룻밤 극기해 보라.
그러면 내일 참기는 한결 쉬워지고
그 다음엔 더더욱 수월해진다.
대저 습관이란
천성을 바꾸어 놓는 법,
비상한 힘이 있어
악마를 굴복시켜 몰아내 버린다.

Chapter 23 Assume a Virtue, If You Have It Not.

Assume a virtue, if you have it not.
That monster custom, who all sense doth eat,
Of habits devil, is angel yet in this,
That to the use of actions fair and good
He likewise gives a frock or livery
That aptly is put on. Refrain tonight,
And that shall lend a kind of easiness
To the next abstinence; the next more easy;
For use almost can change the stamp of nature,
And either [master] the devil, or throw him out
With wondrous potency.

제24장 그대와 그대의 타고난 재능은

그대와 그대의 타고난 재능은
자신의 미덕만을 위해 자신을 소비하고
자신만을 위해 그 미덕을 낭비해도 좋은
그대만의 전유물이 아니다.
우리가 횃불을 사용할 때
횃불 자체를 위해
불을 밝히는 것이 아니듯이,
하늘은 우리를 사용할 때 그와 같이 쓰신다.
만일, 우리의 미덕이
우리 자신에게서 사회적 실천으로
나아가지 않는다면,
그것은 우리가 미덕을
지니고 있지 않은 것과 같은 것이다.
좋은 자질이란
선업을 잘 이루라고 주어진 것이다.
자연이란 여신은
그녀의 위대함의 지극히 적은 양이라도
우리에게 대여해 줄 때는
알뜰히 챙기는 여신답게
채권자의 당연한 권리인 감사와 함께
이자까지 결정지어 놓지 않고는
빌려주지 않는 법이다.

Chapter 24 Thyself and Thy Belongings

Thyself and thy belongings
Are not thine own so proper as to waste
Thyself upon thy virtues, they on thee.
Heaven doth with us as we with torches do,
Not light them for themselves; for if our virtues
Did not go forth of us, 'twere all alike
As if we had them not. Spirits are not finely touched
But to fine issues, nor Nature never lends
The smallest scruple of her excellence
But like a thrifty goddess she determines
Herself the glory of a creditor,
Both thanks and use.

제25장 뜨거운 얼음

참으로 신기한 눈雪인
뜨거운 얼음,
이렇게 모순이 조화되는
불일치의 일치를
어떻게 찾을 수 있겠는가?
오, 다투게 하는 사랑! 사랑하는 미움!
모든 것은 본래 무에서 생겨났다!
육중한 가벼움,
경건한 허무,
그럴 듯하게 형태를 잘 갖춘
보기 흉한 혼돈,
납덩이로 된 깃털,
밝은 그을음,
차가운 불꽃,
병든 건강,
늘 깨어 있는 잠,
이 모두 그것 아닌 그것이다!
이런 것이 사랑이니 사랑을 하면서도
아무런 사랑을 느끼지 못한다.

Chapter 25 Hot Ice

Hot ice and wondrous strange snow.
How shall we find the concord of this discord?
O brawling love, O loving hate.
O anything, of nothing first created!
O heavy lightness, serious vanity,
Misshapen chaos of well-seeming forms,
Feather of lead, bright smoke, cold fire, sick health,
Still-waking sleep, that is not what it is!
This love feel I, that feel no love in this.

제26장 하늘을 대신하여 칼을 드는 사람은

하늘을 대신하여
칼을 드는 사람은
준엄해야 하는 동시에
경건해야 한다.
타인을 판단하는 기준을
자신의 행위에서 알아내고
흔들림 없이 나아갈 수 있는
청렴함과 덕이 있어야 한다.
자신의 죄과의 무게를 달아 보고
결코 그 이상의 것을
다른 사람에게
지불케 해서는 아니 된다.

Chapter 26 He Who the Sword of Heaven Will Bear

He who the sword of heaven will bear
Should be as holy as severe;
Pattern in himself to know,
Grace to stand, and virtue go;
More nor less to others paying
Than by self-offenses weighing.

제27장 인간이란

인간이란
참으로 위대한 걸작품이 아닌가!
이성은 얼마나 고귀하고,
능력은 얼마나 무한하며,
자태와 거동은 얼마나
위엄있고 경탄스러우며
행동은 얼마나 천사 같고,
이해력은 실로 신과 같지 아니한가!
이 지상의 아름다움이고,
만물의 영장이다.
그런데 이러한 인간이건만
내겐 먼지의 먼지로밖에는 보이지 않으니
인간이란 대체 무엇인가?

Chapter 27 Man

What a piece of work is a man, how noble in reason, how infinite in faculties, in form and moving how express and admirable, in action how like an angel, in apprehension how like a god: the beauty of the world, the paragon of animals; and yet to me, what is this quintessence of dust?

제28장 시간의 자녀가 되라

시간의 자녀가 되라.
클레오파트라에게는
모든 것이 잘 어울린다.
화내는 것도, 웃는 것도, 우는 것도,
그녀의 모든 감정은
그녀에게서 나타나면
그 자체가 아름답고 경탄스럽다.
그녀는 세월도 시들게 하지 못하고
도덕적 관습 역시
그녀의 무한한 다양성을
손상시키지 못한다.
다른 여성들은
자신들이 충족시켜주는 욕구를
물리게 하고 말지만
그녀는 그녀에게 최고로 포만감을 느낄 때
굶주림을 느끼게 만들어 버린다.
그녀에게는
가장 부도덕한 일조차 잘 어울려
성직자들도 그녀가 방종할 때
축복을 해 준다.

Chapter 28 Be a Child of the Time

Be a child o' th' time.   [Cleopatra]
Whom everything becomes - to chide, to laugh,
To weep; whose every passion fully strives
To make itself, in [her], fair and admired.
Age cannot wither her, nor custom stale
Her infinite variety: other women cloy
The appetites they feed, but she makes hungry
Where most she satisfies; for vilest things
Become themselves in her, that the holy priests
Bless her when she is riggish.

제29장 우리의 의지와 운명

우리의 의지와 운명은
서로 반대로 가서
우리들이 계획한 바는
늘 뒤집혀지게 마련이다.
우리의 생각은 우리의 것이나
그 결과는 우리 것이 아니다.
때에 따라서는 무분별이
오히려 도움이 된다.
심사숙고한 계획도
수포로 돌아가는 수가 있는 법이니까.
따라서
사람이 웬만큼 손질해 만들어 놓겠지만
결국 다듬어서 완성시키는 것은
하느님이라는 것을 알게 된다.

Chapter 29 Our Wills and Fates

Our wills and fates do so contrary run

That our devices still are overthrown;

Our thoughts are ours, their ends none of our own.

Our indiscretion sometime serves us well

When our deep plots do pall, and that should learn us

There's a divinity that shapes our ends,

Rough-hew them how we will.

제30장 공정한 정의

독보리 심은 곳에
밀이 나지 않는다.
공평한 인과의 수레바퀴는
늘 정확하게 도는 법이다.
살인을 가르치면
가르친 자에게 되돌아간다.
공정한 정의의 손은
독배를 부은 자의 입에
그 독을 도로 부어준다.
권력은 그 자체로는
더없이 격찬 받을 만한 것이지만
그것이 한 일을 떠받들게 하면
그 자리는 무덤이 되고 만다.
불은 다른 불에 의해 꺼지고
못은 다른 못에게 자리를 빼앗기듯이
권력은 권력에게 무너지고
힘은 힘에 의해 패한다.

Chapter 30 Even-handed Justice

Sowed cockle reaped no corn,
And justice always whirls in equal measure.
                              We but teach
Bloody instructions, which, being taught, return
To plague th' inventor: this even-handed justice
Commends th' ingredients of our poisoned chalice
To our own lips.
Power, unto itself most commendable,
Hath not a tomb so evident as a chair
T' extol what it hath done.
One fire drives out one fire; one nail, one nail;
Rights by rights founder, strengths by strengths do fail.

제31장 모든 사람에게 공통된 이름

"호머Homo"는
모든 사람에게 공통된 이름이다.
피 위에 세워진 토대는
견고하지 못하다.
타인의 죽음으로 얻어진 삶은
안전하지 못하다.
피는 피를 부르게 되어 있는 것이다.
인간과 인간은
서로 형제가 되어야 한다.
인간이라는 흙덩어리와 흙덩어리는
세상의 지위에서는 다르지만,
그들은 결국 먼지로서
둘 다 같은 것이다.
우리 모두는
형제처럼 이 세상에 왔으니
이제 손에 손을 잡고
누가 앞이라 할 것 없이
나란히 함께 가야한다.
지상의 온갖 것들이 화해로울 때
하늘에 기쁨이 넘친다.

Chapter 31   A Common Name to All Men.

"Homo" is a common name to all men.
There is no sure foundation set on blood,
No certain life achieved by others' death.
Blood will have blood.
[Brothers] man and man should be,
But clay and clay differs in dignity,
Whose dust is both alike.
We came into the world like brother and brother:
And now let's go hand in hand, not one before another.
Then is there mirth in heaven
When earthly things made even
Atone together.

제32장 세속의 영광

세속의 영광은
마치 물 위의 둥근 파문과 같아서
멈춤이 없이 커져 나가
마침내는 넓게 퍼져서는
사라지고 만다.
사람들은 지는 해를 보고
문을 닫는다.

Chapter 32 Glory

Glory is like a circle in the water,
Which never ceaseth to enlarge itself
Till by broad spreading it disperse to nought.
Men shut their doors against a setting sun.

제33장 나의 왕관

나의 왕관은
마음속에 있지
머리 위에 있지 않다.
그 왕관은
다이아몬드나 인도의 보석으로
장식된 것이 아니고,
눈에 보이지도 않는다.
나의 왕관은
'만족'이라 호칭된다.
그것은
왕들이 좀처럼 갖지 못하는 왕관이다.

Chapter 33 My Crown

My crown is in my heart, not on my head;
Not decked with diamonds and Indian stones,
Nor to be seen. My crown is called content:
A crown it is that seldom kings enjoy.

제34장 인생은 한 번의 숨결

생명이란 무엇인가에 대해 이렇게 생각하라.
내 그대 생명을 잃을지라도 바보들이나 간직하려는
아무 것도 아닌 것을 잃을 따름이라고.
생명, 그대는 한 번의 숨결에 지나지 않는 것,
그대는 하늘의 성신들의 영향력에 굴복할 수밖에 없고
시시각각 고민이 기어드는 일시적인 거처다.
그대는 죽음의 어릿광대,
아무리 죽음을 피해 도망치려 해도
여전히 죽음을 향하여 달음질치게 된다.
생명, 그대는 고상하지 못하다.
그대가 향유하는 안락은 천한 것에서 자라난 것이니까.
그대는 용감하지도 않다.
하찮은 뱀의 연약한 두 갈래 혀를 겁내고 있으니까.
그대의 가장 좋은 안식은 잠자는 것이다.
그런데 때로는 억지로라도 잠을 자려 애쓰면서도
잠에 불과한 죽음을 무척 두려워한다.
생명, 그대는 그대의 것이 아니다.
흙에서 나온 수천가지의 곡식 낟알에 의존하고 있으니까.
그대는 행복하지도 않다.
없으면 얻으려고 악전고투하고
있으면 그만 잊어버리고 마니까.
그대는 한결같지도 않다.

달이 차고 이지러짐에 따라
그대의 몸과 마음은 이상하게 변하니까.
그대는 부유해도 가난한 자다.
금덩어리로 등이 휜 당나귀처럼 무거운 재물을 지고
인생의 여정을 터벅터벅 걸어가다가
죽어서야 겨우 그 짐을 풀어놓게 되니까.
그대는 친한 친구 하나도 없다.
그대를 아버지라고 부르는 자식까지도
그대가 빨리 죽어 없어지지 않는다고
통풍이나 옴, 감기 등을 원망하며 저주하니까.
그대는 청춘도 노년도 없다.
말하자면, 점심 후의 낮잠 같은 것으로
모두 일장춘몽에 불과하다.
그대의 화려한 청춘도 언젠가는 모두 늙게 되어
중풍 걸린 노부모의 재산에 얹혀 살게 되고,
늙어서 부유하게 될 때는 이미 열정도 애정도
아름다움도 다 없어지고 팔다리도 못쓰게 되어
그 재물조차 즐길 수 없게 된다.
이런 것에 생명이라는 이름표를 붙일 수 있겠는가?
이밖에도 수천 가지 죽을 고생이 우리 인생에 숨어있는데
그래도 사람들은 죽음을 겁낸다.
죽음이 이 모든 것을 없애고 평온을 주는데도 말이다.

Chapter 34 Life's But Breath.

                Reason thus with life:
If I do lose thee, I do lose a thing
That none but fools would keep; a breath thou art,
Servile to all the skyey influences,
That dost this habitation, where thou keep'st,
Hourly afflict; merely, thou art death's fool,
For him thou labor'st by thy flight to shun,
And yet run'st toward him still. Thou art not noble,
For all th' accommodations that thou bear'st
Are nursed by baseness. Thou'rt by no means valiant,
For thou dost fear the soft and tender fork
Of a poor worm. Thy best of rest is sleep,
And that thou oft provok'st; yet grossly fear'st
Thy death, which is no more. Thou art not thyself;
For thou exists on many a thousand grains
That issue out of dust. Happy thou art not,
For what thou hast not, still thou striv'st to get,
And what thou hast, forget'st. Thou art not certain,
For thy complexion shifts to strange effects,
After the moon. If thou art rich, thou'rt poor.
For, like an ass whose back with ingots bows,

Thou bear'st thy heavy riches but a journey,
And death unloads thee. Friend hast thou none,
For thine own bowels, which do call thee sire,
The mere effusion of thy proper loins,
Do curse the gout, serpigo, and the rheum,
For ending thee no sooner. Thou hast nor youth nor age,
But, as it were, an after-dinner's sleep,
Dreaming on both; for all thy blessed youth
Becomes as aged, and doth beg the alms
Of palsied eld, and when thou art old and rich,
Thou has neither heat, affection, limb, nor beauty,
To make thy riches pleasant. What's yet in this
That bears the name of life? Yet in this life
Lie hid moe thousand deaths; yet death we fear,
That makes these odds all even.

제35장 야심을 버려라

야심을 버려라.
야심은 천사까지도 타락케 한 죄악이다.
그런데 신의 이미지에 불과한
우리 인간이 어떻게 야심에 의해
천하를 거머쥘 수 있단 말이냐?
너 자신을 맨 나중에 사랑하고
너를 미워하는 사람을 소중히 하라.
부정은 정직을 이기지 못한다.
언제나 바른 손에는
온화한 평화를 가지고 다니면서
시기하는 사람의 입을 다물게 하라.
마음을 의롭게 하고
아무것도 두려워하지 말라.

Chapter 35 Fling Away Ambition.

Fling away ambition.
By that sin fell the angels. How can man then,
The image of his Maker, hope to win by it?
Love thyself last; cherish those hearts that hate thee;
Corruption wins not more than honesty.
Still in thy right hand carry gentle peace
To silence envious tongues. Be just, and fear not.

제36장 그대의 부드러움

힘을 써서
강제로 상냥하게 만드는 것 보다
부드럽게 대하는 것이
더 큰 힘을 발휘한다.
남자들의 세계는
온갖 수사력을 동원한
웅변으로도 잘 돌아가지 않는다.
그러나 한 여인의 부드러운 친절에는
설득당하는 법이다.
부드럽고,
온화하고
나지막한 목소리로 말하는 것,
그것은 여성에게 있는 놀라운 탁월함이다.

Chapter 36 Your Gentleness

Your gentleness shall force
More than your force move us to gentleness.
When a world of men
Could not prevail with all their oratory,
Yet hath a woman's kindness overruled.
Her voice [is] ever soft,
Gentle and low, an excellent thing in woman.

제37장 인생은 걸어가는 그림자

내일, 또 내일, 또 내일,
하루 하루는
이렇게 시시한 발걸음으로
기록된 최후의 순간까지
엉금 엉금 기어들고,
흘러간 모든 어제의 시간들은
우리 바보들에게
한 줌의 흙으로 돌아가는 길을
비추어 보여 주었지.
꺼져라! 꺼져 버려라,
짧은 한 순간의 촛불이여!
인생은 걸어가는 그림자,
자기가 맡은 시간만은
무대 위에서 우쭐대고 안달하지만
그것이 지나면 잊혀지고 마는
가련한 연극배우.
인생은 바보가 지껄이는 이야기,
소리와 분노로 가득하지만
결국 아무 것도 의미하지 않는 이야기.

Chapter 37 Life's But a Walking Shadow.

Tomorrow, and tomorrow, and tomorrow,
Creeps in this petty pace from day to day,
To the last syllable of recorded time;
And all our yesterdays have lighted fools
The way to dusty death. Out, out, brief candle!
Life's but a walking shadow, a poor player
That struts and frets his hour upon the stage
And then is heard no more. It is a tale
Told by an idiot, full of sound and fury
Signifying nothing.

제38장 억지로 뭘 하려는 사람들은

자연은
인간의 매우 고집스러운
인위적인 행위에 대해선
반드시 후회하게 만들어 버린다.
억지로 뭘 하려는 자들에게는
그들 스스로 야기하는 해악이
그들의 스승이 되어야 한다.

Chapter 38 Willful Men

                       Strange it is
That nature must compel us to lament
Our most persisted deeds. To willful men
The injuries that they themselves procure
Must be their schoolmasters.

제39장 죄 없는 사람이라고 해서

불행은
반드시 그 불행을 상속받을
자신의 상속자를
데리고서야 찾아온다.
하나의 불행은
또 다른 불행의
뒤꿈치를 밟고 오며
눈 깜짝할 사이에
따라붙는다.
불행이 찾아 들 때는
혼자서 슬그머니
오는 것이 아니라
대병력으로 밀어닥치는 법이다.
우리가 "이것이 최악이다"라고
말할 수 있는 한
이것은 최악이 아니다.
죄 없는 사람이라고 해서
벼락을 면하는 것은 아니다.

Chapter 39 Some Innocents

One sorrow never comes but brings an heir
That may succeed as his inheritor.
One woe doth tread upon another's heel,
So fast they follow.
When sorrows come, they come not single spies,
But in battalions. The worst is not
So long as we can say, "This is the worst."
Some innocents 'scape not the thunderbolt.

제40장 그 반대로 되돌아간다

어느 것도
한결 같이 좋게만 계속되지 않는다.
좋음이 지나침에 이르면
그 자신의 과도함으로 인해
스러지게 된다.
좋음이 지나치면
나쁨으로 전환된다.
최상의 상태에서
변화가 생기는 것은 안타까운 일이나
최악에 달한 비극은
웃음으로 되돌아온다.
모든 것은
그 반대로 되돌아가는 법이다.

Chapter 40 The Opposite of Itself

Nothing is at a like goodness still,
For goodness, growing to a plurisy,
Dies in his own too-much.
Thy overflow of good converts to bad.
The lamentable change is from the best,
The worst returns to laughter.
All things change them to the contrary.

제41장 진정한 일꾼

나는 진정한 일꾼이다.
내 스스로 일해서 먹고,
내 손으로 벌어서 입고,
남의 미움도 사지 않으며,
남의 행복을 시샘하지 않으며,
남의 좋은 일을 기뻐하며,
나의 어려움은 잘 참는다.
그리고 나의 가장 큰 자랑은
암양들이 풀을 뜯어 먹고
새끼 양들이 엄마 젖을 빠는 것을
바라보는 것이다.
타인의 잘남을 개의치 말라.
태어나면서부터 잘 난 사람이 있고,
힘써 노력하여 잘 난 사람도 있고,
또한 남이 시켜주어
잘나게 된 사람도 있는 것이다.
그리고 죄악으로 출세하는 자도 있고
미덕으로 인해 몰락하는 자도 있는 것이다.

Chapter 41 A True Laborer

I am a true laborer; I earn that I eat, get
that I wear, owe no man hate, envy no man's happiness,
glad of other men's good, content with my harm;
and the greatest of my pride is to see my ewes graze
and my lambs suck. Be not afraid of greatness.
Some are born great, some achieve greatness, and
some have greatness thrust upon 'em.
[And] some rise by sin, and some by virtue fall.

제42장 텅 비어 널리 편재해 떠도는 대기

우리는 어느 땐
용처럼 생긴 구름을 보게 된다.
어느 때는 구름이
곰이나 사자 같기도 하고.
우뚝 솟은 성채,
떨어질 듯이 매달린 바위,
갈라진 산, 또는 수목들이 뒤덮인
험준한 푸른 곶 같은 모양을 하고는
인간세를 내려다보며 허공 속에서
대기로 우리의 눈을 조롱한다.
이러한 형상들은 모두
땅거미 밀려오는
저녁나절에 보이는 광경이다.
지금 말馬로 보이는 것이
홀연히 그 구름이 지워지면서
물이 물속에 있듯이 희미해져 버린다.
지금의 그대 역시
바로 그러한 몸일 뿐,
지금의 가시적인 모습을
그대로 지탱해 갈 수는 없는 것이다.

Chapter 42   The Empty, Vast, and Wand'ring Air

Sometime we see a cloud that's dragonish,

A vapor sometime like a bear or lion,

A towered citadel, a pendant rock,

A forked mountain, or blue promontory

With trees upon't that nod unto the world

And mock our eyes with air.

Thy are black vesper's pageants.

That which is now a horse, even with a thought

The rack dislimns, and makes it indistinct

As water is in water. Now [thou art]

Even such a body,

Yet cannot hold this visible shape.

제43장 세속에서 벗어난 숲속의 삶

자연의 숲속에선
아담의 형벌인 계절의 변화를
느끼지 않는다.
한겨울 차가운 바람의 어금니와
매서운 채찍질이 살을 에듯
우리 몸에 불어와
온 몸이 추워 오그라들 때도
난 웃으며 말한다:
"이것은 아첨이 아니다. 이들은 내가 누구인지
온몸으로 배우게 해 주는 충언자들이다."
고난의 이로움은 아름답다.
고난은 두꺼비처럼
흉측하고 독이 들어 있지만
그 머리에는 귀한 보석이 씌어져 있다.
세속의 번잡함에서 벗어난
자연에서의 생활은
나무가 하는 말을 듣고,
흐르는 개울이 읊어주는 책을 읽고,
돌멩이로부터 설교를 듣는가 하면
모든 것에서
선을 발견하게 된다.

Chapter 43 Our life, Exempt from Public Haunt

[In these woods] feel we not the penalty of Adam;
The seasons' difference, as the icy fang
And churlish chiding of the winter's wind,
Which, when it bites and blows upon my body
Even till I shrink with cold, I smile and say,
"This is no flattery; these are counselors
That feelingly persuade me what I am."
Sweet are the uses of adversity,
Which, like the toad, ugly and venomous,
Wears yet a precious jewel in his head;
And this our life, exempt from public haunt,
Finds tongues in trees, books in the running brooks,
Sermons in stones, and good in everything.

제44장 명예란 무엇이냐?

명예가
떨어져 나간 다리를
복구시켜 주는가?
아니다.
그럼 팔은?
역시 아니다.
혹은 상처의 아픔을
가시게 해주는가?
어림없는 일이다.
그럼 명예랍시고
외과 의사만큼의 수완도
안 가졌는가?
그렇다.
그럼 명예란 도대체 무엇인가?
한낱 말에 불과하다.
그럼 명예라는 말에는 대체 뭐가 있는가?
대관절 이 명예란 무엇이란 말인가?
공기일 뿐이다.

Chapter 44 What is honor?

Can honor set to a leg? No. Or an arm? No.
Or take away the grief of a wound? No.
Honor had no skill in surgery then? No.
What is honor? A word. What is in that word honor?
What is that honor? Air.

제45장 인성의 한 가지 공통성

시간이란
유행을 쫓는 여관의 주인 같아서
떠나가는 손님에겐
손을 조금 흔들지만
새로 오는 손님에게는
양팔을 벌리고 달려가 맞이한다.
환영할 때는 늘 미소를 짓지만
이별할 때는 한숨을 내쉰다.
덕이 과거에 대해
보답을 구하지 않도록 하라.
아름다움도, 사랑도, 우정도, 자선도,
이 모두가 시기하고 비방하는
시간에는 못 견딘다.
우리 인성의 한 가지 공통점이
온 세계를 일가친척으로 만들어 준다.
그것은 별 대단치도 않지만
새로 나온 물건은
죄다 찬사를 한다는 점이다.
새 것이라 한들
과거의 것을 바탕으로
만들었는데도 말이다.
먼지에 쌓인 황금보다는
황금빛 씌운 먼지를 더 칭찬하게 마련이다.

Chapter 45 One Touch of Nature

Time is like a fashionable host,
That slightly shakes his parting guest by the hand,
And with his arms outstretched, as he would fly,
Grasps in the comer. The welcome ever smiles,
And farewell goes out sighing. Let not virtue seek
Remuneration for the thing it was. For beauty, wit,
High birth, vigor of bone, desert in service,
Love, friendship, charity, are subjects all
To envious and calumniating time.
One touch of nature makes the whole world kin,
That all with one consent praise newborn gauds,
Though they are made and molded of things past,
And give to dust that is a little gilt
More laud than gilt o'erdusted.

제46장 큰 부자

가난해도
만족하는 사람은
부자도 큰 부자이다.
그러나
엄청난 부자라 해도
곧 가난뱅이가 되는 것이
아닌가 하고 늘 걱정한다면,
그 사람은 가난하기가
엄동설한 같은 것이다.
가난한 부자는
가득 쌓인 부富속에
들어앉아서도
가난해지기 때문에,
남아돌아 싫증이 나면서도
더욱 더 많은 것을
갈망하게 된다.

Chapter 46 Rich Enough

Poor and content is rich, and rich enough;
But riches fineless is as poor as winter
To him that ever fears he shall be poor.
But poorly rich, so wanteth in his store
That, cloyed with much, he pineth still for more.

제47장 이 세상은 하나의 무대

이 세상은 하나의 무대,
모든 남녀는 연극배우에 불과한 것,
등장하는가 하면 퇴장하고
일생동안 맡아 하는 많은 역할은
7 막으로 나뉜다.
처음엔 갓난아기,
유모 품에 안겨 칭얼대며 보챈다.
그 다음은 투덜대는 어린 학생,
빛나는 아침얼굴로 가방을 메고
달팽이처럼 느릿느릿 가기 싫은 학교를
마지못해 억지로 걸어간다.
그리고는 연인,
용광로처럼 한숨을 몰아쉬며
연인의 눈썹을 그리며
애처로운 발라드를 짓는다.
그러고 나면 군인,
엉뚱한 호언장담만을 늘어놓고
수염은 표범모양을 한 채
명예욕에 불타,
걸핏하면 핏대 올려 싸우려 들면서
물거품 같은 명예를 위해서라면
대포 아가리 속에도 서슴치 않고 뛰어든다.

그 뒤엔 법관,
두둑한 뇌물에 배는 기름져 피둥피둥,
매서운 눈초리에 수염은 격식대로 기르고
격언이나 상투적인 실례만 늘어놓는
그런 역할을 한다.
여섯 번째 막은
슬리퍼를 신은 말라빠진
바보 늙은이로 옮겨간다.
콧잔등엔 안경을 걸치고
허리춤엔 돈주머니를 차고
잘 아껴둔 젊은 시절의 바지는
마른 정강이에 비해 너무 통이 커 진
세상이 되어 버리고,
그 사나이답던 굵은 목소리는
어린애 목소리로 돌아가
피리소리나 휘파람소리를 내게 된다.
파란 많은 이 인생의 드라마를 마감하는
마지막 장은 제 2의 유아기,
철저한 망각만이 남아
이도 빠지고,
눈도 보이지 않고,
입맛도 없어지면서
세상만사가 그저 허망해 진다.

Chapter 47 All the World's a Stage.

All the world's a stage,
And all the men and women merely players;
They have their exits and their entrances,
And one man in his time plays many parts,
His acts being seven ages. At first, the infant,
Mewling and puking in the nurse's arms.
Then the whining schoolboy, with his satchel
And shining morning face, creeping like snail
Unwillingly to school. And then the lover,
Sighing like furnace, with a woeful ballad
Made to his mistress' eyebrow. Then a soldier,
Full of strange oaths and bearded like the pard,
Jealous in honor, sudden and quick in quarrel,
Seeking the bubble reputation
Even in the cannon's mouth. And then the justice,
In fair round belly with good capon lined,
With eyes severe and beard of formal cut,
Full of wise saws and modern instances;
And so he plays his part. The sixth age shifts

Into the lean and slippered pantaloon,
With spectacles on nose and pouch on side;
His youthful hose, well saved, a world too wide
For his shrunk shank, and his big manly voice,
Turning again toward childish treble, pipes
And whistles in his sound. Last scene of all,
That ends this strange eventful history,
Is second childishness and mere oblivion,
Sans teeth, sans eyes, sans taste, sans everything.

제48장 스스로 그러한대로 되게 하라

참새 한 마리가 떨어지는 데도
특별한 섭리가 있는 법이다.
와야 할 때가 지금이라면
앞으로 오지 않을 것이고,
오지 않을 것이면
지금이 그때이다.
때가 지금이 아니라면
때는 오기는 할 것이고.
늘 준비가 되어 있으면 되는 것이다.
어느 누구도
자기가 무엇을 남기고 떠나는지 모르는데,
일찍 떠난다 한들 무엇이 아쉽겠는가?
스스로 그러한 대로 되어가도록 하라.

Chapter 48 Let It Be

There is special providence in the fall of a sparrow. If it be now, 'tis not to come; if it be not to come, it will be now; if it be not now, yet it will come. The readiness is all. Since no man of aught he leaves knows, what is't to leave betimes? Let be.

제49장 정치는 음악처럼

정치라는 것은
상위와 하위, 최하위로 나뉘지만
모든 구성원들이 참여하여
음악처럼
하나의 거대한 조화를 이루며
풍요롭고 자연스러운
화음을 이루어가야 한다.

Chapter 49 Government Like Music

Government, though high, low, and lower,
Put into parts, doth keep in one consent,
Congreeing in a full and natural close,
Like music.

제50장 삶의 고요한 완성

태양의 타오르는 뜨거움도
혹독한 겨울의 추위도
이제 더 이상 두려워 말라.
그대는 세상 일 다 끝냈고
집은 사라지고 그대의 삯을 받았으니.
선남선녀들 모두 굴뚝 청소부와 다름없이
흙으로 돌아가야 하는 것.

힘 있는 자의 찡그린 얼굴을
이제 더는 겁내지 말라.
그대는 폭군의 폭력을 벗어났으니.
입을 것 먹을 것 더 이상 걱정 말라.
그대에겐 갈대도 참나무와 다름없으니.
왕이나 학자나 의사 이 모두들
이처럼 흙으로 돌아가야 하는 것.

번갯불도 모두가 겁내는 번개화살도
이제는 무서워 말라.
헐뜯는 중상이나 무모한 비난도 두려워 말라.
그대는 기쁨과 신음 모두 끝내었으니.
모든 젊은 연인들, 모든 연인들
그대 따라 흙으로 돌아가야 하는 것.

어떤 무당도 그대를 해치지 못하리라.
어떤 마법도 그대에게 마술을 걸지 못하리라.
유령도 그대를 조용히 놓아두리라.
불길한 것은 그대 가까이 오지 못하리라.

삶의 고요한 완성을 이루니
그대의 무덤 널리 알려지리라.

Chapter 50 Quiet Consummation

Fear no more the heat o' th' sun
  Nor the furious winter's rages;
Thou thy worldly task hast done,
  Home art gone and ta'en thy wages.
Golden lads and girls all must,
As chimney-sweepers, come to dust.

Fear no more the frown o' th' great;
  Thou are past the tyrant's stroke.
Care no more to clothe and eat;
  To thee the reed is as the oak.
The scepter, learning, physic, must
All follow this and come to dust.

Fear no more the lightning flash,
   Nor th' all-dreaded thunder-stone;
Fear not slander, censure rash;
   Thou hast finished joy and moan.
All lovers young, all lovers must
Consign to thee and come to dust.

No exorciser harm thee,
Nor no witchcraft charm thee.
Ghost unlaid forbear thee;
Nothing ill come near thee.

Quiet consummation have,
And renowned be thy grave.

제51장 지금 이 순간 속의 미래

인생이란
숨 한 번 쉬는 것에 불과하고
"하나"라고 말하기도 전에 끝난다.
그러나
나는 지금 이 순간 속에 들어 있는
미래를 느낀다.
영원이라는 시간은
우리가 현재 이 순간 하고 있는
입맞춤과 주고받는 눈길 속에 있는 것이다.
그러므로
삶의 단 한 순간도
즐거움이 없이 보내져서는 아니 된다.

Chapter 51 The Future in the Instant

Life's but breath.
A Man's life's no more than to say "one."
[But] I feel now
The future in the instant.
Eternity [is] in our lips and eyes.
[And so] there's not a minute of our lives should stretch
Without some pleasure now.

제52장 지옥으로 이끄는 천국

정욕을 행하는 것은
수치스러운 낭비로
정신을 소모하는 것이다.
행할 때까지 정욕은 위증이고,
살인적이고, 잔인하고, 힐난으로 가득 차
야만적이고, 과격하고, 거칠며,
잔혹하여 믿을 것이 못된다.
향락이 끝나면 곧 경멸이고,
이성을 지나쳐 추구하고
그것을 얻자마자
이성을 지나쳐 혐오하게 된다.
마치 먹는 자를 미치게 하기 위해
고의로 놓은 미끼를 삼키는 것과 같다.
추구하는 동안에도 광증이고,
소유한 뒤에도 광증이며,
행한 뒤에도, 행하고 있는 중에도,
행하려 하는 동안에도 극단이다.
경험 중에는 축복이고, 경험 뒤에는 비애다.
그 전에는 환희를 주나 그 후에는 악몽을 남긴다.
세상 사람들 이 모든 것을 잘 알지만,
이런 지옥으로 사람을 이끄는 천국을
피하는 것은 아무도 잘 알지 못한다.

Chapter 52 The Heaven that Leads Men to Hell

Th' expense of spirit in a waste of shame
Is lust in action; and, till action, lust
Is perjured, murd'rous, bloody, full of blame,
Savage, extreme, rude, cruel, not to trust;
Enjoyed no sooner but despised straight;
Past reason hunted, and no sooner had,
Past reason hated as a swallowed bait
On purpose laid to make the taker mad;
Made in pursuit, and in possession so;
Had, having, and in quest to have, extreme;
A bliss in proof, and proved, a very woe,
Before, a joy proposed; behind, a dream.
All this the world well knows, yet none knows well
To shun the heaven that leads men to this hell.

제53장 하늘의 도가 공평함을

무자비한 폭풍우를
견디며 사는
헐벗고 가난한 사람들,
어디에 있든
머리 둘 집도 없고
배는 굶주리고
창문처럼 구멍 난
누더기 옷을 걸치고
어떻게 폭풍우의
험한 날씨를 견디며
살 수 있다는 말인가!
부귀영화를
누리고 있는 자들이여,
좋은 약이니
이런 것을 경험해 보라.
없이 사는 사람들의 처지를
너희 스스로 느껴 볼 수 있도록
폭풍우를 맞아 보고
너희의 남은 것을
그들에게 나누어 주어
하늘의 도가 공평함을
보여 주어라.

Chapter 53 The Heavens More Just

Poor naked wretches, wheresoe'er you are,
That bide the pelting of this pitiless storm,
How shall your houseless heads and unfed sides,
Your looped and windowed raggedness, defend you
From [tempest]. Take physic, pomp;
Expose thyself to feel what wretches feel,
That thou mayst shake the superflux to them,
And show the heavens more just.

제54장 덕 있는 행위

부정한 얻음이
나쁜 결과를 초래한다는 말을
듣지 못했는가?
재산 축적 때문에
지옥에 떨어진 아버지의 이야기를 듣고
아들이 행복해 하더라는 말을
들은 적이 없는가?
아들에게 덕행을 물려주라.
덕 이외의 것은
그것을 유지하기 위하여
소유하는 기쁨보다
천 배 많은 근심을 초래하기 때문이다.
덕이 있으면 용감하게 되고
선하면 두려워하지 않게 된다.

Chapter 54 Virtuous Deeds

      Didst you never hear
That things ill got had ever bad success?
And happy always was it for that son
Whose father for his hoarding went to hell?
Leave [thy] son [thy] virtuous deeds behind.
For all the rest is held at such a rate
As brings a thousandfold more care to keep
Than in possession any jot of pleasure.
Virtue is bold, and goodness never fearful.

제55장 그대가 춤을 출 때면

그대가 춤을 출 때면
난 그대가
바다의 물결이기를 바란다.
그저 언제까지나
조용히 움직이는가 하면
움직이며 고요히
그 외에는 어떤 작용도 없이 그렇게.
그대가 하는 일은
그 무엇이든 독특해서
현재 하는 행위에 왕관을 씌우니
그대의 모든 행위는
그 자체로 여왕들이 된다.

Chapter 55 When You Do Dance

When you do dance, I wish you
A wave o' th' sea, that you might ever do
Nothing but that - move still, still so,
And own no other function. Each your doing,
So singular in each particular,
Crowns what you are doing in the present deeds,
That all your acts are queens.

제56장 훌륭한 성직자

좋은 일을 실천하는 것이
그것을 아는 것만큼 쉽다면
작은 예배당도 큰 교회가 되었을 것이고
가난한 사람들의 오두막도
왕후의 궁전이 되었을 것이다.
자신이 한 설교를 행동으로 옮기는 사람은
훌륭한 성직자다.
자신이 가르친 좋은 일을 실천하는
스무 사람 중의 한 사람이 되기보다는
그 스무 사람을 가르치는 게
훨씬 쉬운 법이다.
세상에 흔히 있는
저 파렴치한 목사들처럼,
남에겐 험한 가시밭길을
천국에 가는 길이라고 가르쳐 주면서,
정작 자신은 허풍이나 떨고
분별없는 짓이나 일삼는 방탕꾼처럼
환락의 꽃밭 길을 거닐면서
자기가 한 설교는 거들떠보지도 않는
그런 짓은 하지 말라.
사람이 제대로 된 사람이어야 하고
하는 일이 올바른 것이어야지
사제복만 입었다고 성직자가 되는 것은 아니다.

Chapter 56 A Good Divine

If to do were as easy as to know what were good
to do, chapels had been churches, and poor men's
cottages princes' palaces. It is a good divine that
follows his own instructions; I can easier teach
twenty what were good to be done, than to be one
of the twenty to follow mine own teaching.
Do not, as some ungracious pastors do,
Show me the steep and thorny way to heaven,
Whiles, like a puffed and reckless libertine,
Himself the primrose path of dalliance treads,
And recks not his own rede.
They should be good men, their affairs as righteous;
But all hoods make not monks.

제57장 오만한 인간은

오만한 인간은
일시적인 자그마한 권력을
맡아 가지고 있는 것에 불과한데도
자기가 유리같이 깨지기 쉬운
취약한 존재라는 뻔한 사실도 알지 못하고
성난 원숭이 같이
드높은 하늘 앞에서
별의별 괴상한 농간을 다 부려
천사들을 울려놓는다.
오만한 인간은
자기 자신을 잡아먹는 법이다.
오만이란 자신의 거울이고, 나팔이고, 기록이다.
자신이 한 일을 자화자찬하다가
그 한 일 조차 잡아먹고 만다.

Chapter 57 Proud Man

                Man, proud man,
Dressed in a little brief authority,
Most ignorant of what he's most assured,
His glassy essence, like an angry ape,
Plays such fantastic tricks before high heaven
As makes the angels weep.
He that is proud eats up himself.
Pride is his own glass, his own trumpet, his own chronicle;
and whatever praises itself but in the deed, devours the
deed in the praise.

제58장 슬픔이 기뻐하고, 기쁨이 슬퍼한다

결심이란
단지 기억의 노예일 뿐이다.
태어날 땐 맹렬하나
그 힘이란 미약하다.
열매가 설익었을 땐
나무에 단단히 달려있지만,
익게 되면 그냥 둬도
저절로 떨어지는 법이다.
우리가 자신에게 빚진 것을 잊어버려
못 갚는 건 도저히 피할 수가 없는 것이다.
격정 속에 자신에게 제안한 것은
그 격정이 사라지면 결심조차 없어진다.
기쁨이나 슬픔이 과도하면
그 행위에 의해 자기 자신을
사그라지게 한다.
기쁨이 한껏 즐기는 곳에는
슬픔이 가장 비통해 한다.
사소한 일에도
슬픔이 기뻐하고
기쁨이 슬퍼한다.

Chapter 58 Grief Joys, Joy Grieves.

Purpose is but the slave to memory,
Of violent birth, but poor validity,
Which now like fruit unripe sticks on the tree,
But fall unshaken when they mellow be.
Most necessary 'tis that we forget
To pay ourselves what to ourselves is debt.
What to ourselves in passion we propose,
The passion ending, doth the purpose lose.
The violence of either grief or joy
Their own enactures with themselves destroy:
Where joy most revels, grief doth most lament;
Grief joys, joy grieves, on slender accident.

제59장 삶이라는 직물

인간의 삶은
좋음과 나쁨의 올이
서로 섞여 직조된 직물이다.
덕이 잘못에게
매를 맞지 않는다면
덕도 방자해 질 것이고,
우리의 죄도
덕이 감싸 주지 않으면
절망하고 말 것이다.

Chapter 59 The Web of Our Life

The web of our life is of a mingled yarn,
good and ill together; our virtues would be proud if
our faults whipped them not, and our crimes would
despair if they were not cherished by our virtues.

제60장 아무리 미천한 곳에서라도

인간들의 피는
모두 쏟아 놓고 보면
그 색깔, 무게, 온도에는
아무런 차이가 없는데도
큰 차이가 있는 것처럼 구별되는 것은
이상한 일이다.
아무리 미천한 곳에서라도
유덕한 일이 일어나면
그 유덕한 행위를 행한 사람 때문에
그곳은 존귀하게 된다.
지위만 높고 덕이 없으면
그것은 병든 명예일 뿐이다.
좋음은 이름이 없어도
그 자체로 좋은 것이다.
나쁨도 마찬가지다.
본성 그대로의 특성은
이름 없이도 그대로 나타나는 법이다.

Chapter 60 From Lowest Place

                      Strange is it that our bloods,
Of color, weight, and heat, poured all together,
Would quite confound distinction, yet stands off
In differences so mighty.
From lowest place when virtuous things proceed,
The place is dignified by th' doer's deed.
Where great additions swell's and virtue none,
It is a dropsied honor. Good alone
Is good, without a name; vileness is so:
The property by what it is should go,
Not by the title.

제61장 평화의 하모니

화의를 통한 평화는
본질적으로 정복한 승리와 같은 것이다.
양쪽이 용기 있게 낮춤으로써
서로가 잃는 것이 없기 때문이다.
[영국 왕 심벨린은 로마와의 전쟁에서
승리했음에도 다음과 같이 선포한다]:
"짐은 평화를 열어 가고자 하노라.
내 비록 승리자이긴 하나
로마황제에게 자세를 낮추어
관례대로 조공을 바치기로 하노라."
이는 하늘의 기운이
평화의 화음을 연주하는 것이고
당당한 독수리라 할 로마 황제가
찬란한 심벨린 왕과 우의를 다시 하여
서쪽 나라 영국에서 빛나는 것이다.

Chapter 61 The Harmony of Peace

A peace is of the nature of a conquest,
For then both parties nobly are subdued.
And neither party loser.
"My peace we will begin.
Although the victor, we submit to Caesar
And to the Roman empire, promising
To pay our wonted tribute."
The fingers of the pow'rs above do tune
The harmony of this peace.
[And] our princely eagle,
Th' imperial Caesar, should again unite
His favor with the radiant Cymbeline,
Which shines here in the west.

제62장 악한 것에 깃든 선한 혼

악한 것에도
뭔가 선의 혼이 깃들어 있는 법이다.
그 선을 잘 증류해 내야한다.
나쁜 이웃은
우리를 일찍 일어나게 해서
건강하고 검소한 생활을 하게 한다.
그들은 우리의 외면적인 양심이고,
목적을 위해 단단히 준비하라고 이르는
설교자이기도 하다.
이렇게 잡초에서도 꿀을 따고
악마에게서도 도덕적 교훈을
얻을 수가 있는 것이다.

Chapter 62 Soul of Goodness in Things Evil

There is some soul of goodness in things evil,
Would men observingly distill it out;
For our bad neighbour makes us early stirrers,
Which is both healthful, and husbandry.
Besides, they are our outward consciences,
And preachers to us all, admonishing
That we should dress us fairly for our end.
Thus may we gather honey from the weed,
And make a moral of the devil himself.

제63장 큰 불을

급히 큰 불을
일으키려는 사람도
보잘 것 없는 한 올의 지푸라기로
불을 피우기 시작한다.

Chapter 63 Mighty Fire

**Those that with haste will make a mighty fire
Begin it with weak straws.**

제64장 작은 불꽃은

작은 불꽃은
불면 곧 꺼지지만,
큰 불은
타기를 계속하고
바람이 불면
더 맹렬히 타오른다.
작은 모닥불은
밟아 뭉개어 쉽게 끌 수 있지만
그 불도
그냥 놔두면
강물로도 끄지 못한다.

Chapter 64   Small Lights

Small lights are soon blown out; huge fires abide
And with the wind in greater fury fret.
A little fire is quickly trodden out;
Which, being suffered, rivers cannot quench.

제65장 우리 자신에게 무지하니

우리는
우리 자신에 대해 무지해서
흔히 우리 자신에게
해악이 되는 것을
간절히 구한다.
현명한 신들이 우리를 위해
그것을 거부하는데도 말이다.
우리가
이 세상에 태어날 때
울어 대는 것은
바보들로 득실대는
이 거대한 무대에 왔다고 해서
우는 것이다.

Chapter 65 Ignorant of Ourselves

We, ignorant of ourselves,
Beg often our own harms, which the wise pow'rs
Deny us for our good.
When we are born, we cry that we are come
To this great stage of fools.

제66장 군주란

군주란 거울이고, 학교이며, 책이다.
거기에서 백성들의 눈은
보고 읽고 배운다.
군주란 하늘을 닮도록
하늘이 세워 놓은 모범이다.
보석도 경시되면 눈부신 아름다움을 잃듯이,
군주도 존경 받지 못하면 명망을 잃고 만다.

Chapter 66   Princes

Princes are the glass, the school, the book,
Where subjects' eyes do learn, do read, do look.
                              Princes are
A model which heaven makes like to itself:
As jewels lose their glory if neglected,
So princes their renowns if not respected.

제67장 가장 좋은 사람

모든 사람을 사랑하되
소수의 사람을 믿고
아무에게도
해를 끼치지 말 것이며
적을 감당할 능력을 갖추되
그 힘을 사용하지 말고
친구는
네 인생의 해답을 줄 수 있는
열쇠라 생각하고 사귀어라.
침묵 때문에
비난받을 지라도
말이 많은 것 때문에
책망 받지 않도록 하라.
말이 거의 없는 사람이
가장 좋은 사람이다.

Chapter 67 The Best Men

Love all, trust a few,
Do wrong to none; be able for thine enemy
Rather in power than use, and keep thy friend
Under thy own life's key. Be checked for silence,
But never taxed for speech.
Men of few words are the best men.

제68장 적에게 분노하지 마라

적에게 과열하게
분노의 불을 지피면
자신이 화상을 입게 된다.
너무 맹렬한 속력을 내면
목표 지점을 지나치게 되어
맹렬하게 달린 만큼의 손해를 보게 된다.
물이 끓어 넘치도록 불을 지피면
그 양은 불어난 것 같이 보이지만
실제로는 줄어드는 것을 알지 못하는가?

Chapter 68 Heat Not a Furnace for Your Foe.

Heat not a furnace for your foe so hot
That it do singe yourself. We may outrun
By violent swiftness that which we run at,
And lose by overrunning. Know you not
The fire that mounts the liquor till't run o'er
In seeming to augment it wastes it?

제69장 장군의 장군

상관이 없을 때 큰 공적을 세워
지나친 명성을 떨치느니보다는
차라리 안 하고 마는 것이
안전하다는 것을 알아두라.
전쟁에서 지휘 장군 이상의
공로를 세우는 자는
지휘 장군의 지휘 장군이 된다.
그렇게 되면 무인의 공명심이란
자기의 명예를 무색하게 하는 승리보다는
차라리 패배를 택하는 법이다.

Chapter 69 Captain's Captain

Better to leave undone, than by our deed
Acquire too high a fame when him we serve's away.
Who does i' th' wars more than his captain can
Becomes his captain's captain; and ambition
(The soldier's virtue) rather makes choice of loss
Than gain which darkens him.

제70장 더러운 굴껍질 속에 진주가 있듯이

바다에는
물고기가 살고 있다.
눈에 보이는 아름다움은
눈에 보이지 않는 아름다움을
그 속에 감추고 있는 것이
큰 자랑이다.
풍요로운 덕성은
구두쇠처럼 산다.
진주가 더러운 굴껍질 속에
간직되어 있듯이,
보잘 것 없는 집에
살고 있다.

Chapter 70 As Your Pearl in Your Foul Oyster.

The fish lives in the sea, and 'tis much pride
For fair without the fair within to hide.
Rich honesty dwells like a miser, in a poor
house as your pearl in your foul oyster.

제71장 말을 삼가라

가진 것을 다 보이지 말고
알고 있어도 말을 삼가고
가진 것 이상으로 꾸어주지 말라
말을 탈 수 있을 때 걷지 말며
알고 있는 것보다 더 많이 배우며
따서 번 것보다는 적게 걸고
주색을 멀리하라.

Chapter 71 Speak Less

Have more than thou showest,
Speak less than thou knowest,
Lend less than thou owest,
Ride more than thou goest,
Learn more than thou trowest,
Set less than thou throwest;
Leave thy drink and thy whore.

제72장 우주의 늑대

힘은 옳아야 한다.
그렇지 않으면,
옳음과 그름은
그 이름을 잃어야 하고
이 둘 사이의 끊임없는 다툼에 놓이는
정의마저도 이름을 잃어야 한다.
그리되면
만물은 자신을 힘으로 포장하게 되고
힘은 의지로 바뀌고,
의지는 다시 욕심으로 바뀌어
우주의 늑대인 그 욕심은
의지와 힘을 이중으로 업고
필연적으로 우주의 먹이가 되어
마침내 자기 자신을 먹어 치우게 된다.

Chapter 72   Universal Wolf

Force should be right, or rather right and wrong -
Between whose endless jar justice resides -
Should lose their names, and so should justice too.
Then everything include itself in power,
Power into will, will into appetite,
And appetite, an universal wolf,
So doubly seconded with will and power,
Must make perforce an universal prey
And last eat up himself.

제73장 마음을 편히 하고 인내심을 품고 살라

마음을 편히 하고
인내심을 품고 살라.
아무리 으르렁대는 슬픔도
그것을 비웃고 아무렇지도 않게
생각하는 사람은
물어뜯지 못하는 법이다.
그리고
지나간 불행을 슬퍼하는 것은
바로 새로운 불행을 불러들인다.
운명이 간직 할 수 없는 것을
빼앗아 갈 때는
잘 참고 견디는 것만이 그 타격을
비웃을 수 있다.
빼앗긴 자가 미소를 지으면
빼앗아 가는 자로부터
도로 빼앗아 올 수 있지만
쓸데없는 슬픔에 잠기면
자기 자신을 빼앗기고 만다.
바다가 잔잔할 때에는
어떤 사공이라도
다 같이 배를 저어 낼 수 있지만,
운명의 극심한 타격을 받고도
의연하게 참고 있으려면
높은 인격이 필요하다.

Chapter 73 Bear Free and Patient Thoughts.

Bear free and patient thoughts.
The gnarling sorrow hath less power to bite
The man that mocks at it and sets it light.
[And] to mourn a mischief that is past and gone
Is the next way to draw new mischief on.
What cannot be preserved when fortune takes,
Patience her injury a mock'ry makes.
The robbed that smiles, steals something from the thief;
He robs himself that spends a bootless grief.
When the sea [is] calm all boats alike
[Show] mastership in floating; fortune's blows
When most struck home, being gentle wounded craves
A noble cunning.

제74장 평온을 주는 죽음

이 모든것에 싫증이 나서
나는 평온한 죽음을 갈망한다.
거지의 천성을 타고난 사람이 훌륭한 사람으로 보여 지게 되고,
그리고 무일푼의 형편없는 인간이 화려하게 단장하고
그리고 순수한 신념이 위증으로 비참하게 욕을 당하고
그리고 찬란한 명예가 부끄럽게도 엉뚱한 사람에게 주어지고
그리고 순결한 정조가 무참하게 유린당하게 되고
그리고 완전무결한 것이 부당하게 더럽힘 받게 되고
그리고 건전한 힘이 무능한 권력에게 꺾이게 되고
그리고 예술이 권력에 의해 벙어리가 되고
그리고 어리석은 자가 의사인양 숙련을 좌우하게 되고
그리고 순수한 진실이 어리석음으로 불리우고
그리고 악의 손에 떨어진 선이 악에게 시중들고 있으니.
이 같은 모든 일들에 싫증이 나서 나는 죽고 싶다.
죽는 것이 내 사랑만을 남겨 두고 가는 것이 아니라면.

Chapter 74 Restful Death

Tired with all these, for restful death I cry,
As, to behold desert a beggar born,
And needy nothing trimmed in jollity,
And purest faith unhappily forsworn,
And gilded honor shamefully misplaced,
And maiden virtue rudely strumpeted,
And right perfection wrongfully disgraced,
And strength by limping sway disabled,
And art made tongue-tied by authority,
And folly (doctorlike) controlling skill,
And simple truth miscalled simplicity,
And captive good attending captain ill.
Tired with all these, from these would I be gone,
Save that to die, I leave my love alone.

제75장 보잘 것 없는 이득

욕심이 많은 자들은
얻는 것에만 탐욕하게 되어
소유하고 있으면서도
누리지 못하고
제 손에서 떠나게 하여 잃고 만다.
그리고
더 많은 것을 얻고 싶어 하나
오히려 잃기만 한다.
바라는 대로 많이 얻는다 해도
과도한 이득은 과식에 불과하고
그로 인해 고통이 지속되어
보잘 것 없는 이득 때문에
파멸에 이른다.
원하는 것을 얻는다 해서
무슨 소득이 있겠는가?
그것은 꿈이고, 순간의 입김이고,
덧없는 즐거움의 거품일 뿐이다.
누가 일주일의 울부짖는 회한을 지불하고
한순간의 환락을 사고자하며
하잘 것 없는 장난감 하나 얻자고 영원을 팔겠는가?
누가 달콤한 포도 한 알을 얻으려고
덩굴을 모두 망치려 하겠는가?

어리석은 거지라 할지라도
왕관을 한 번 만져볼 수 있다면
그 즉석에서 왕 홀에 맞아 죽어도 좋다는 자가
어디 있겠는가?

Chapter 75 Poor Rich Gain

Those that much covet are with gain so fond
That what they have not, that which they possess
They scatter and unloose it from their bond,
And so by hoping more they have but less,
Or, gaining more, the profit of excess
Is but to surfeit, and such griefs sustain
That they prove bankrout in this poor rich gain.
What win I if I gain the thing I seek?
A dream, a breath, a froth of fleeting joy.
Who buys a minute's mirth to wail a week?
Or sells eternity to get a toy?
For one sweet grape who will the vine destroy?
Or what fond beggar, but to touch the crown,
Would with the scepter straight be stroken down?

제76장 맹렬한 불은

맹렬한 불같이
난폭하고 성급한 성격은
오래 지속되지 못한다.
맹렬한 불은
스스로 빨리 타 버리니까.
작은 빗발은 오래 가지만
갑자기 내리는 폭우는 짧고
너무 급히 말을 모는 자는
빨리 지친다.

Chapter 76 Violent Fires

His rash fierce blaze of riot cannot last,
For violent fires soon burn out themselves.
Small showers last long, but sudden storms are short;
He tires betimes that spurs too fast betimes.

제77장 고결한 마음

아무것도 아닌 것을
대견하게 보아줄 줄 알면
우리는 더욱 친절한 사람들이다.
남의 실수를 용인해 주는 것도
즐거움이라 할 수 있다.
마음이 고결한 사람은
아랫사람이 서투른 솜씨로
정성껏 해서 안 되는 경우
그 애쓴 마음만을 취하고
결과는 불문에 붙인다.
만일 사람을
그 사람의 가치에 따라 대접한다면
이 세상에 회초리를 맞지 않을 사람이
누가 있겠는가?
그러므로
그대의 명예와 인품에 어울리게 대접하라.
상대방에 그만한 자격이 없으면 없을수록
이쪽의 후한 선심이 더욱 빛나는 법이다.

Chapter 77 Noble Respect

The kinder we, to give them thanks for nothing.
Our sport shall be to take what they mistake:
And what poor duty cannot do, noble respect
Takes it in might, not merit.
Use every man after his desert, and who shall
scape whipping? Use them after your own honor
and dignity. The less they deserve, the more
merit is in your bounty.

제78장 덕과 지식은

덕과 지식은
사회적 지위나 재산보다도
더 소중한 자산이다.
자식이 방탕이라도 하면,
지위는 더럽혀지고
재산은 탕진되고 만다.
그러나
덕과 지식은 불멸하고
그걸 몸에 지닌 사람을
신으로 만들어 준다.
부질없이 명예를 갈망하거나
비단 자루에 재화를 모아 보았자
광대와 염라대왕의
조롱감밖에는 되지 않는다.

Chapter 78 Virtue and Cunning

Virtue and cunning [are] endowments greater
Than nobleness and riches: careless heirs
May the two latter darken and expend,
But immortality attends the former,
Making a man a god.
To be thirsty after tottering honor,
Or tie my treasure up in silken bags, [is]
To please the Fool and Death.

제79장 유일한 피스메이커

두 사람 사이에
싸움이 벌어졌는데
판사 일곱이 달려들어
화해를 시키려 해도
소용이 없었다.
그래서 드디어 결투까지 이르러
두 사람이 마주 서게 되었는데
그중 한 사람이
마침 "만약에"라고
한마디 덧붙일 생각이 나서
"당신이 만약 이리이리 말했다면
나는 이리이리 말했을 거요"라고 말했다.
그래서 그 두 사람은
악수하고 의형제를 맺었다.
싸움의 중재역으로는
이 "만약에"라는 놈 이상이 없다.
"만약에" 속에는
대단한 화해력이 들어 있다.

Chapter 79 The Only Peacemaker

I knew when seven justices could not take up a quarrel, but when the parties were met themselves, one of them thought but of an If: as, "If you said so, then I said so"; and they shook hands and swore brothers. Your If is the only peacemaker. Much virtue in If.

제80장 새 공화국에서는

새로운 공화국에선 무슨 일이든지
지금까지와는 정 반대로 할 것이다.
어떠한 교통수단도 허락하지 않을 것이고,
관료의 직함도 없고
문자도 알려주지 않을 것이다.
부와 가난, 하인의 부림도 없고,
계약, 상속, 경계, 토지의 구획,
경작, 포도밭도 없으며,
금속, 곡물, 술, 기름의 사용은 물론
직업도 없게 할 것이다.
모든 남자들은 그저 한가로이 지내며
여자들도 한가롭기는 마찬가지다.
하지만 순수하고 무욕하다.
군주권이라는 것도 없을 것이다.
자연의 품안에 있는 만물은
땀과 노력 없이도 잘 자라니
모반, 중죄, 창검, 칼, 총을 비롯해
어떤 무기도 필요치 않게 할 것이다.
그러나 자연은 모든 풍작과 풍요로움을 가져와
순진무구한 백성을 먹여 살릴 것이다.

Chapter 80 In the Commonwealth

I' th' commonwealth I would by contraries
Execute all things. For no kind of traffic
Would I admit; no name of magistrate;
Letters should not be known; riches, poverty,
And use of service, none; contract, succession,
Bourn, bound of land, tilth, vineyard, none;
No use of metal, corn, or wine, or oil;
No occupation; all men idle, all;
And women too, but innocent and pure;
No sovereignty.
All things in common nature should produce
Without sweat or endeavor. Treason, felony,
Sword, pike, knife, gun, or need of any engine
Would I not have; but nature should bring forth,
Of it own kind, all foison, all abundance,
To feed my innocent people.

제81장　내가 주면 줄수록

말을 한다고
말이 되는 게 아니라
진실하게 말하는 것이 중요하다.
행동을 말에,
말을 행동에 일치시켜라.
특별히 명심해야 할 것은
자연의 절도를 넘지 않도록 하라.
말로 헤아릴 수 있는 사랑은
빈궁한 것이다.
사랑의 한계를 그어보고자 하면
새로운 하늘, 새로운 땅을
찾아야 할 것이다.
나의 넉넉함은
바다와 같이 끝이 없고
사랑도 마찬가지로 깊고 깊다.
내가 주면 줄수록
내가 더욱 더
풍요롭게 된다.

Chapter 81 The More I Give to Thee

It is not enough to speak, but to speak true.
Suit the action to the word, the word to the action,
with this special observance, that you o'erstep not
the modesty of nature.
There's beggary in the love that can be reckoned.
[To] set a bourn how far to be beloved,
Must thou needs find out new heaven, new earth.
My bounty is as boundless as the sea,
My love as deep; the more I give to thee,
The more I have.

참고한 책과 자료

1. 셰익스피어 작품 영어 전집

Shakespeare, William. *The Complete Signet Classic Shakespeare.*
　　ed. Sylvan Barnet. New York: Harcourt, 1972.
_____. *The Riverside Shakespeare.* ed. G. Blakemore Evans.
　　New York: Houghton, 1977.

2. 셰익스피어 작품 한글 번역 서적

셰익스피어, 윌리엄. 『셰익스피어 全集』. 1-4권. 여석기 외 다수 역. 서울: 정음사, 1980.
_____. 『셰익스피어 全集』. 김재남 역. 서울: 을지서적, 1995.
_____. 『셰익스피어 전집』. 이상섭 역. 서울: 문학과 지성사, 2016.
_____. 『셰익스피어 전집』. 1-8권. 최종철 역. 서울: 민음사, 2016.
_____. 『소네트』. 정종화 옮김. 서울: 민음사, 1988.
_____. 『셰익스피어 소네트의 이해』. 신영수 지음. 서울: 한신문화사, 2000.

3. 셰익스피어 문구 모음집

Lamb, G.F. *The Wordsworth Dictionary of Shakespeare Quotations.*
　　Hertfordshire: 1995.
Mary and Foakes, Reginald. *The Columbia Dictionary of Quotations*
　　From Shakespeare. New York: Barnes, 2000.
박성환. 편집. 『셰익스피어의 위대한 문장들』. 파주: 문학동네, 2007.
한광석. 『굿모닝 셰익스피어』. 고양: 해토, 2007.

4. 노자 『도덕경』

김용옥. 『노자 길과 얻음』. 서울: 통나무, 1990.
____. 『노자와 21세기』. 서울: 통나무, 2000.
____. 『노자가 옳았다』. 서울: 통나무, 2020.
김학주. 역주. 『초원 이충익의 담노 역주』. 통나무: 2014.
임채우. 번역. 『왕필의 노자』. 서울: 예문서원, 1997.
Lao Tzu. *Tao Te Ching. A Source Book in Chinese Philosophy*. Translated and compiled by Wing-Tsit Chan. Princeton: Princeton UP, 1973: 139-176.
Wang Pi. *Commentary on the Lao Tzu*. Trans. Ariane Rump and Wing-Tsit Chan. Honolulu: U of Hawaii P, 1979.

Appendix
『셰익스피어의 도덕경 그린월드』의 셰익스피어 작품 출처

Shakespeare's New Bible of The Way and Its Virtue

Green World

Chapter 1 Love, and Be Silent.

Love, and be silent. (*King Lear* 1.1.62)

[True love] cannot speak;
For truth hath better deeds than words to grace it.
    (*The Two Gentlemen of Verona* 2.2.17-18)

Truth hath a quiet breast. (*Richard II* 1.3.96)

Truth should be silent. (*Antony and Cleopatra* 2.2.108)

'Tis but [the name of Romeo Montague] that is [Juliet's] enemy.
[He is himself], though not a Montague.
What's Montague? It is nor hand, nor foot,
Nor arm, nor face, nor any other part
Belonging to a man. O, be some other name.
What's in a name? That which we call a rose
By any other word would smell as sweet.
So Romeo would, were he not Romeo called,
Retain that dear perfection which he owes
Without that title. (*Romeo and Juliet* 2.2.38-47)

Chapter 2 Fair Is Foul.

Fair is foul, and foul is fair. (*Macbeth* 1.1.10)

There is nothing either good or bad,
but thinking makes it so. (*Hamlet* 2.2.254)

"Ay" and "no" too [is] no good divinity. (*King Lear* 4.6.98)

Chapter 3 A Witty Fool

Better a witty fool than a foolish wit. (*Twelfth Night* 1.5.36)

                Folly, in wisdom hatched,
Hath wisdom's warrant and the help of school
And wit's own grace to grace a learned fool.
            (*Love's Labor's Lost* 5.2.70-72)

Folly in fools bears not so strong a note
As fool'ry in the wise when with doth dote.
            (*Love's Labor's Lost* 5.2.75-76)

Folly that [the fool] wisely shows, is fit;
But wise men, folly-fall'n, quite taint their wit.
            (*Twelfth Night* 3.1.68-9)

Chapter 4 A Local Habitation and a Name to Airy Nothing

The lunatic, the lover, and the poet
Are of imagination all compact.
One sees more devils than vast hell can hold,
That is the madman. The lover, all as frantic,
Sees Helen's beauty in a brow of Egypt.
The poet's eye, in a fine frenzy rolling,
Doth glance from heaven to earth, from earth to heaven;
And as imagination bodies forth
The forms of things unknown, the poet's pen
Turns them to shapes, and gives to airy nothing
A local habitation and a name.
            (*A Midsummer Night's Dream* 5.1.7-17)

Chapter 5 Divine Nature (*Cymbeline* 4.2.170)

The self-same sun that shines upon his court
Hides not his visage from our cottage, but
Looks on alike. (*The Winter's Tale* 4.4.447-49)

Our dungy earth alike
Feeds beast as man. (*Antony and Cleopatra* 1.1.35-6)

Nature should bring forth,
Of it own kind, all foison, all abundance,
To feed my innocent people. (*The Tempest* 2.1.167-169)

Chapter 6 Nature's Mother

The earth that's Nature's mother is her tomb.
What is her burying grave, that is her womb.
And from her womb children of divers kind
We sucking on her natural bosom find,
Many for many virtues excellent,
None but for some, and yet all different.
O, mickle is the powerful grace that lies
In plants, herbs, stones, and their true qualities;
For naught so vile that on the earth doth live
But to the earth some special good doth give;
Nor aught so good but, strained from that fair use,
Revolts from true birth, stumbling on abuse.
Virtue itself turns vice being misapplied,
And vice sometime by action dignified.
                              (*Romeo and Juliet* 2.3.9-22)

Chapter 7 The Lord of His Face

They that have pow'r to hurt and will do none,
That do not do the thing they most do show,
Who, moving others, are themselves as stone,
Unmoved, cold, and to temptation slow;
They rightly do inherit heaven's graces
And husband nature's riches from expense;
They are the lords and owners of their faces,
Others but stewards of their excellence.
The summer's flow'r is to the summer sweet,
Though to itself it only live and die;
But if that flow'r with base infection meet,

The basest weed outbraves his dignity:
  For sweetest things turn sourest by their deeds;
  Lilies that fester smell far worse than weeds.
                    (*The Sonnets* 94)

Chapter 8 The Man That's Not Passion's Slave

One, in suff'ring all, that suffers nothing,
A man that Fortune's buffets and rewards
Hast ta'en with equal thanks; and blest are those
Whose blood and judgment are so well commeddled
That they are not a pipe for Fortune's finger
To sound what stop she please. Give me that man
That is not passion's slave, and I will wear him
In my heart's core, ay, in my heart of heart. (*Hamlet* 3.2.65-72)

Chapter 9 Modest Wisdom (*Macbeth* 4.3.119)

            The sweetest honey
Is loathsome in his own deliciousness
And in the taste confounds the appetite.
      (*Romeo and Juliet* 2.6.11-13)

They are as sick that surfeit with too much as they
that starve with nothing. It is not mean happiness, therefore,
to be seated in the mean; superfluity comes sooner
by white hairs, but competency lives longer.
      (*The Merchant of Venice* 1.2.5-8)

The crow doth sing as sweetly as the lark
When neither is attended; and I think
The nightingale, if she should sing by day
When every goose is cackling, would be thought
No better a musician than the wren.
How many things by season, seasoned are
To their right praise and true perfection!
      (*The Merchant of Venice* 5.1.102-108)

Chapter 10 Birth and Heaven and Earth

Birth and heaven and earth, all three do meet
In thee at once. (*Romeo and Juliet* 3.3.120-121)

'Tis in ourselves that we are thus, or thus.
Our bodies are our gardens, to the which our
wills are gardeners; so that if we will plant nettles or
sow lettuce, set hyssop and weed up thyme, supply it
with one gender of herbs or distract it with many –
either to have it sterile with idleness or manured with
industry – why, the power and corrigible authority
of this lies in our wills. (*Othello* 1.3.314-321)

Frame your mind to mirth and merriment,
Which bars a thousand harms and lengthens life.
    (*The Taming of The Shrew* Induction. ii. 134-135)

Chapter 11   The Quality of Nothing (*King Lear* 1.2.33)

Can you make no use of nothing? (*King Lear* 1.4.132)

    Nothing is
But what is not. (*Macbeth* 1.3.141)

Nothing brings me all things. (*Timon of Athens* 5.1.188)

Nor I, nor any man that but man is,
With nothing shall be pleased, till he be eased
With being nothing. (*Richard II* 5.5.39-41)

Chapter 12   The Error of our Eye

The error of our eye directs our mind.
What error leads must err. . . .
Minds swayed by eyes are full of turpitude.
      (*Troilus and Cressida* 5.2.107-109)

By our ears our hearts oft tainted be.
      (*The Rape of Lucrece* 38)

Chapter 13   The Mystery of Things (*King Lear* 5.3.16)

From that spring whence comfort seemed to come
Discomfort swells. (*Macbeth* 1.2.27-28)

Good wombs have borne bad sons. (*The Tempest* 1.2.119)

Sweet love, I see, changing his property,
Turns to the sourest and most deadly hate.
     (*Richard II* 3.2.135-6)

    The present pleasure,
By revolution low'ring, does become
The opposite of itself. (*Antony and Cleopatra* 1.2.125-127)

Chapter 14 The Rarest Dream (*Pericles* 5.1.165)

        I have had a most rare
vision. I have had a dream, past the wit of man to say
what dream it was. Man is but an ass, if he go about
to expound this dream. Methought I was – there is no
man can tell what. Methought I was – and methought
I had – but man is but a patch'd fool, if he will offer
to say what methought I had. The eye of man hath not
heard, the ear of man hath not seen, man's hand is
not able to taste, his tongue to conceive, nor his heart
to report, what my dream was.
  (*A Midsummer Night's Dream* 4.1.205-214)

Chapter 15 To Be, or Not To Be

To be, or not to be: that is the question:
Whether 'tis nobler in the mind to suffer
The slings and arrows of outrageous fortune,
Or to take arms against a sea of troubles,

And by opposing end them. To die, to sleep –
No more – and by a sleep to say we end
The heartache, and the thousand natural shocks
That flesh is heir to! 'Tis a consummation
Devoutly to be wished. To die, to sleep –
To sleep – perchance to dream: ay, there's the rub,
For in that sleep of death what dreams may come
When we have shuffled off this mortal coil,
Must give us pause. There's the respect
That makes calamity of so long life:
For who would bear the whips and scorns of time,
Th' oppressor's wrong, the proud man's contumely,
The pangs of despised love, the law's delay,
The insolence of office, and the spurns
That patient merit of th' unworthy takes,
When he himself might his quietus make
With a bare bodkin? Who would fardels bear,
To grunt and sweat under a weary life,
But that the dread of something after death,
The undiscovered country, from whose bourn
No traveler returns, puzzles the will,
And makes us rather bear those ills we have,
Than fly to others that we know not of?
Thus conscience does make cowards of us all,
And thus the native hue of resolution
Is sicklied o'er with the pale cast of thought,
And enterprises of great pitch and moment,
With this regard their currents turn awry,
And lose the name of action. (*Hamlet* 3.1.56-88)

Chapter 16 A Good Voyage of Nothing (*Twelfth Night* 2.4.78)

Alexander died, Alexander was buried, Alexander returneth
to dust; the dust is earth; of earth we make loam;
and why of that loam whereto he was converted might
they not stop a beer barrel?
Imperious Caesar, dead and turn'd to clay,
Might stop a hole to keep the wind away.
O, that that earth which kept the world in awe
Should patch a wall t' expel the winter's flaw!
                    (*Hamlet* 5.1.209-16)

Chapter 17 Ripeness Is All.

Ripeness is all. (*King Lear* 5.2.11)

[Crocodile] is shaped, sir, like itself, and it is as broad as it hath
 breadth; it is just so high as it is, and moves with it own organs.
It lives by that which nourisheth it, and the elements once out of it,
 it transmigrates. . . . Of it own color too.
                    (*Antony and Cleopatra* 2.7.42-48)

Chapter 18 The Man That Hath No Music in Himself

                                        The poet
Did feign that Orpheus drew trees, stones, and floods;
Since naught so stockish, hard, and full of rage
But music for the time doth change his nature.
The man that hath no music in himself,

Nor is not moved with concord of sweet sounds,
Is fit for treason, stratagems, and spoils;
The motions of his spirit are dull as night,
And his affections dark as Erebus.
Let no such man be trusted.
 (*The Merchant of Venice* 5.1.79-88)

Chapter 19 We Fat Ourselves for Maggots.

Your worm is your only emperor for diet. We fat
all creatures else to fat us, and we fat ourselves for
maggots. Your fat king and your lean beggar is but
variable service - two dishes, but to one table. . . .
A man may fish with the worm that hath
eat of a king, and eat of the flesh that hath fed of that
worm. . . . A king may go to progress
through the guts of a beggar. (*Hamlet* 4.3.21-32)

Chapter 20 Study, - So Won, So Lost.

Study is like the heaven's glorious sun,
That will not be deep-searched with saucy looks.
Small have continual plodders ever won
Save base authority from others' books.
These earthly godfathers of heaven's lights,
That give a name to every fixed star
Have no more profit of their shining nights
Than those that walk and wot not what they are.
 (*Love's Labor's Lost* 1.1.84-91)

Study evermore is overshot.
While it doth study to have what it would,
It doth forget to do the thing it should;
And when it hath the thing it hunteth most,
'Tis won as towns with fire - so won, so lost.
   (*Love's Labor's Lost* 1.1.141-145)

Chapter 21 All Shall Dissolve into Thin Air.

   Our revels [will be] ended.
These our actors [are] all spirits and
Are melted into air, into thin air;
And, like the baseless fabric of this vision,
The cloud-capped towers, the gorgeous palaces,
The solemn temples, the great globe itself,
Yea, all which it inherit, shall dissolve,
And, like this insubstantial pageant faded,
Leave not a rack behind. We are such stuff
As dreams are made on, and our little life
Is rounded with a sleep. (*The Tempest* 4.1.148-158)

Chapter 22 The Quality of Mercy

The quality of mercy is not strained;
It droppeth as the gentle rain from heaven
Upon the place beneath. It is twice blest;
It blesseth him that gives and him that takes.
'Tis mightiest in the mightiest; it becomes

The throned monarch better than his crown.
His scepter shows the force of temporal power,
The attribute to awe and majesty,
Wherein doth sit the dread and fear of kings;
But mercy is above this scept'red sway;
It is enthroned in the hearts of kings,
It is an attribute to God Himself,
And earthly power doth then show likest God's
When mercy seasons justice.
　　　　　(*The Merchant of Venice* 4.1.183-196)

Chapter 23 Assume a Virtue, If You Have It Not.

Assume a virtue, if you have it not.
That monster custom, who all sense doth eat,
Of habits devil, is angel yet in this,
That to the use of actions fair and good
He likewise gives a frock or livery
That aptly is put on. Refrain tonight,
And that shall lend a kind of easiness
To the next abstinence; the next more easy;
For use almost can change the stamp of nature,
And either [master] the devil, or throw him out
With wondrous potency. (*Hamlet* 3.4.161-71)

Chapter 24 Thyself and Thy Belongings

　　　　　Thyself and thy belongings
Are not thine own so proper as to waste

Thyself upon thy virtues, they on thee.
Heaven doth with us as we with torches do,
Not light them for themselves; for if our virtues
Did not go forth of us, 'twere all alike
As if we had them not. Spirits are not finely touched
But to fine issues, nor Nature never lends
The smallest scruple of her excellence
But like a thrifty goddess she determines
Herself the glory of a creditor,
Both thanks and use. (*Measure for Measure* 1.1.29-40)

Chapter 25 Hot Ice

Hot ice and wondrous strange snow.
How shall we find the concord of this discord?
    (*A Midsummer Night's Dream* 5.1.59-60)

O brawling love, O loving hate.
O anything, of nothing first created!
O heavy lightness, serious vanity,
Misshapen chaos of well-seeming forms,
Feather of lead, bright smoke, cold fire, sick health,
Still-waking sleep, that is not what it is!
This love feel I, that feel no love in this.
               (*Romeo and Juliet* 1.1.179-85)

Chapter 26 He Who the Sword of Heaven Will Bear

He who the sword of heaven will bear

Should be as holy as severe;
Pattern in himself to know,
Grace to stand, and virtue go;
More nor less to others paying
Than by self-offenses weighing.
   (*Measure for Measure* 3.2.262-267)

Chapter 27 Man

What a piece of work is a man, how noble in reason,
how infinite in faculties, in form and moving how
express and admirable, in action how like an angel,
in apprehension how like a god: the beauty of the world,
the paragon of animals; and yet to me, what is this
quintessence of dust? (*Hamlet* 2.2.311-316)

Chapter 28 Be a Child of the Time

Be a child o' th' time. (*Antony and Cleopatra* 2.7.101)

                  [Cleopatra]
Whom everything becomes - to chide, to laugh,
To weep; whose every passion fully strives
To make itself, in [her], fair and admired.
   (*Antony and Cleopatra* 1.1.48-51)

Age cannot wither her, nor custom stale
Her infinite variety: other women cloy
The appetites they feed, but she makes hungry

Where most she satisfies; for vilest things
Become themselves in her, that the holy priests
Bless her when she is riggish.
    (*Antony and Cleopatra* 2.2.237-42)

Chapter 29 Our Wills and Fates

Our wills and fates do so contrary run
That our devices still are overthrown;
Our thoughts are ours, their ends none of our own.
    (*Hamlet* 3.2.215-217)

Our indiscretion sometime serves us well
When our deep plots do pall, and that should learn us
There's a divinity that shapes our ends,
Rough-hew them how we will. (*Hamlet* 5.2.8-11)

Chapter 30 Even-handed Justice

Sowed cockle reaped no corn,
And justice always whirls in equal measure.
   (*Love's Labor's Lost* 4.3.380-381)

       We but teach
Bloody instructions, which, being taught, return
To plague th' inventor: this even-handed justice
Commends th' ingredients of our poisoned chalice
To our own lips. (*Macbeth* 1.7.8-12)

Power, unto itself most commendable,
Hath not a tomb so evident as a chair
T' extol what it hath done.
One fire drives out one fire; one nail, one nail;
Rights by rights founder, strengths by strengths do fail.
(*Coriolanus* 4.7.51-55)

Chapter 31 A Common Name to All Men.

"Homo" is a common name to all men. (*1 Henry IV* 2.1.96)

There is no sure foundation set on blood,
No certain life achieved by others' death.
(*King John* 4.2.104-105)

Blood will have blood. (*Macbeth* 3.4.122)

[Brothers] man and man should be,
But clay and clay differs in dignity,
Whose dust is both alike. (*Cymbeline* 4.2.4-6)

We came into the world like brother and brother:
And now let's go hand in hand, not one before another.
(*The Comedy of Errors* 5.1.426-427)

Then is there mirth in heaven
When earthly things made even
Atone together. (*As You Like It* 5.4.108-110)

Chapter 32 Glory

Glory is like a circle in the water,
Which never ceaseth to enlarge itself
Till by broad spreading it disperse to nought.
            (*1 Henry VI* 1.2.133-35)

Men shut their doors against a setting sun.
            (*Timon of Athens* 1.2.145)

Chapter 33 My Crown

My crown is in my heart, not on my head;
Not decked with diamonds and Indian stones,
Nor to be seen. My crown is called content:
A crown it is that seldom kings enjoy.
            (*3 Henry VI* 3.1.62-65)

Chapter 34 Life's But Breath. (*Pericles* 1.1.47)

        Reason thus with life:
If I do lose thee, I do lose a thing
That none but fools would keep; a breath thou art,
Servile to all the skyey influences,
That dost this habitation, where thou keep'st,
Hourly afflict; merely, thou art death's fool,
For him thou labor'st by thy flight to shun,
And yet run'st toward him still. Thou art not noble,
For all th' accommodations that thou bear'st

Are nursed by baseness. Thou'rt by no means valiant,
For thou dost fear the soft and tender fork
Of a poor worm. Thy best of rest is sleep,
And that thou oft provok'st; yet grossly fear'st
Thy death, which is no more. Thou art not thyself;
For thou exists on many a thousand grains
That issue out of dust. Happy thou art not,
For what thou hast not, still thou striv'st to get,
And what thou hast, forget'st. Thou art not certain,
For thy complexion shifts to strange effects,
After the moon. If thou art rich, thou'rt poor.
For, like an ass whose back with ingots bows,
Thou bear'st thy heavy riches but a journey,
And death unloads thee. Friend hast thou none,
For thine own bowels, which do call thee sire,
The mere effusion of thy proper loins,
Do curse the gout, serpigo, and the rheum,
For ending thee no sooner. Thou hast nor youth nor age,
But, as it were, an after-dinner's sleep,
Dreaming on both; for all thy blessed youth
Becomes as aged, and doth beg the alms
Of palsied eld, and when thou art old and rich,
Thou has neither heat, affection, limb, nor beauty,
To make thy riches pleasant. What's yet in this
That bears the name of life? Yet in this life
Lie hid moe thousand deaths; yet death we fear,
That makes these odds all even.
             (*Measure for Measure* 3.1.6-41)

Chapter 35 Fling Away Ambition.

> Fling away ambition.
> By that sin fell the angels. How can man then,
> The image of his Maker, hope to win by it?
> Love thyself last; cherish those hearts that hate thee;
> Corruption wins not more than honesty.
> Still in thy right hand carry gentle peace
> To silence envious tongues. Be just, and fear not.
> *(Henry VIII* 3.2.441-447)

Chapter 36 Your Gentleness

> Your gentleness shall force
> More than your force move us to gentleness.
> *(As You Like It* 2.7.102-103)

> When a world of men
> Could not prevail with all their oratory,
> Yet hath a woman's kindness overruled.
> *(1 Henry VI* 2.2.48-50)

> Her voice was ever soft,
> Gentle and low, an excellent thing in woman.
> *(King Lear* 5.3.274-275)

Chapter 37 Life's But a Walking Shadow

Tomorrow, and tomorrow, and tomorrow,

Creeps in this petty pace from day to day,
To the last syllable of recorded time;
And all our yesterdays have lighted fools
The way to dusty death. Out, out, brief candle!
Life's but a walking shadow, a poor player
That struts and frets his hour upon the stage
And then is heard no more. It is a tale
Told by an idiot, full of sound and fury
Signifying nothing. (*Macbeth* 5.5.19-28)

Chapter 38 Willful Men

　　　　　　　　　　Strange it is
That nature must compel us to lament
Our most persisted deeds.
　(*Antony and Cleopatra* 5.1.27-29)

　　　　　　　　　　To willful men
The injuries that they themselves procure
Must be their schoolmasters.
　　　　　(*King Lear* 2.4.299-301)

Chapter 39 Some Innocents

One sorrow never comes but brings an heir
That may succeed as his inheritor. (*Pericles* 1.4.63-64)

One woe doth tread upon another's heel,
So fast they follow. (*Hamlet* 4.7.163-164)

When sorrows come, they come not single spies,
But in battalions. (*Hamlet* 4.5.79-80)

                         The worst is not
So long as we can say, "This is the worst."
             (*King Lear* 4.1.28-29)

Some innocents 'scape not the thunderbolt.
           (*Antony and Cleopatra* 2.5.77)

Chapter 40 The Opposite of Itself (*Antony and Cleopatra* 1.2.127)

Nothing is at a like goodness still,
For goodness, growing to a plurisy,
Dies in his own too-much. (*Hamlet* 4.7.116-18)

Thy overflow of good converts to bad. (*Richard II* 5.3.63)

The lamentable change is from the best,
The worst returns to laughter. (*King Lear* 4.1.5-6)

All things change them to the contrary. (*Romeo and Juliet* 4.5.90)

Chapter 41 A True Laborer

I am a true laborer; I earn that I eat, get
that I wear, owe no man hate, envy no man's happiness,
glad of other men's good, content with my harm;

and the greatest of my pride is to see my ewes graze
and my lambs suck. (*As You Like It* 3.2.72-76)

Be not afraid of greatness. Some are born great,
some achieve greatness, and some have greatness
thrust upon 'em. (*Twelfth Night* 2.5.140-142)

Some rise by sin, and some by virtue fall.
        (*Measure for Measure* 2.1.38)

Chapter 42 The Empty, Vast, and Wand'ring Air (*Richard III* 1.4.39)

Sometime we see a cloud that's dragonish,
A vapor sometime like a bear or lion,
A towered citadel, a pendant rock,
A forked mountain, or blue promontory
With trees upon't that nod unto the world
And mock our eyes with air. Thou hast seen these signs:
Thy are black vesper's pageants. . .
That which is now a horse, even with a thought
The rack dislimns, and makes it indistinct
As water is in water. Now [thou art]
Even such a body,
Yet cannot hold this visible shape.
        (*Antony and Cleopatra* 4.14.2-14)

Chapter 43 Our life, Exempt from Public Haunt

[In these woods] feel we not the penalty of Adam;
The seasons' difference, as the icy fang
And churlish chiding of the winter's wind,
Which, when it bites and blows upon my body
Even till I shrink with cold, I smile and say,
"This is no flattery; these are counselors
That feelingly persuade me what I am."
Sweet are the uses of adversity,
Which, like the toad, ugly and venomous,
Wears yet a precious jewel in his head;
And this our life, exempt from public haunt,
Finds tongues in trees, books in the running brooks,
Sermons in stones, and good in everything.
                            (*As You Like It* 2.1.5-17)

Chapter 44 What is Honor?

Can honor set to a leg? No. Or an arm? No.
Or take away the grief of a wound? No.
Honor had no skill in surgery then? No.
What is honor? A word. What is in that word honor?
What is that honor? Air. (*1 Henry IV* 5.1.131-35)

Chapter 45 One Touch of Nature

Time is like a fashionable host
That slightly shakes his parting guest by the hand,

And with his arms outstretched, as he would fly,
Grasps in the comer. The welcome ever smiles,
And farewell goes out sighing. Let not virtue seek
Remuneration for the thing it was. For beauty, wit,
High birth, vigor of bone, desert in service,
Love, friendship, charity, are subjects all
To envious and calumniating time.
One touch of nature makes the whole world kin,
That all with one consent praise newborn gauds,
Though they are made and molded of things past,
And give to dust that is a little gilt
More laud than gilt o'erdusted.
             (*Troilus and Cressida* 3.3.165-178)

Chapter 46 Rich Enough

Poor and content is rich, and rich enough;
But riches fineless is as poor as winter
To him that ever fears he shall be poor.
             (*Othello* 3.3.172-174)

But poorly rich, so wanteth in his store
That, cloyed with much, he pineth still for more.
             (*The Rape of Lucrece* 97-98)

Chapter 47 All the World's a Stage.

             All the world's a stage,
And all the men and women merely players;

They have their exits and their entrances,
And one man in his time plays many parts,
His acts being seven ages. At first, the infant,
Mewling and puking in the nurse's arms.
Then the whining schoolboy, with his satchel
And shining morning face, creeping like snail
Unwillingly to school. And then the lover,
Sighing like furnace, with a woeful ballad
Made to his mistress' eyebrow. Then a soldier,
Full of strange oaths and bearded like the pard,
Jealous in honor, sudden and quick in quarrel,
Seeking the bubble reputation
Even in the cannon's mouth. And then the justice,
In fair round belly with good capon lined,
With eyes severe and beard of formal cut,
Full of wise saws and modern instances;
And so he plays his part. The sixth age shifts
Into the lean and slippered pantaloon,
With spectacles on nose and pouch on side;
His youthful hose, well saved, a world too wide
For his shrunk shank, and his big manly voice,
Turning again toward childish treble, pipes
And whistles in his sound. Last scene of all,
That ends this strange eventful history,
Is second childishness and mere oblivion,
Sans teeth, sans eyes, sans taste, sans everything.
                    (*As You Like It* 2.7.138-165)

Chapter 48 Let It Be (*Twelfth Night* 1.5.206)

There is special providence in the fall of a sparrow. If it be now, 'tis not to come; if it be not to come, it will be now; if it be not now, yet it will come. The readiness is all. Since no man of aught he leaves knows, what is't to leave betimes? Let be.
(Hamlet 5.2.221-226)

Chapter 49 Government Like Music

Government, though high, low, and lower,
Put into parts, doth keep in one consent,
Congreeing in a full and natural close,
Like music. (*Henry V* 1.2.180-183)

Chapter 50 Quiet Consummation

Fear no more the heat o' th' sun
 Nor the furious winter's rages;
Thou thy worldly task hast done,
 Home art gone and ta'en thy wages.
Golden lads and girls all must,
As chimney-sweepers, come to dust.

Fear no more the frown o' th' great;
 Thou are past the tyrant's stroke.
Care no more to clothe and eat;
 To thee the reed is as the oak.
The scepter, learning, physic, must

All follow this and come to dust.

Fear no more the lightning flash,
   Nor th' all-dreaded thunder-stone;
Fear not slander, censure rash;
   Thou hast finished joy and moan.
All lovers young, all lovers must
Consign to thee and come to dust.

No exorciser harm thee,
Nor no witchcraft charm thee.
Ghost unlaid forbear thee;
Nothing ill come near thee.

Quiet consummation have,
And renowned be thy grave. (*Cymbeline* 4.2.258-281)

Chapter 51 The Future in the Instant

Life's but breath. (*Pericles* 1.1.47)

A Man's life's no more than to say "one." (*Hamlet* 5.2.74)

       I feel now
The future in the instant. (*Macbeth* 1.557-58)

Eternity was in our lips and eyes. (*Antony and Cleopatra* 1.3.35)

There's not a minute of our lives should stretch
Without some pleasure now. (*Antony and Cleopatra* 1.1.46-47)

Chapter 52 The Heaven that Leads Men to Hell

Th' expense of spirit in a waste of shame
Is lust in action; and, till action, lust
Is perjured, murd'rous, bloody, full of blame,
Savage, extreme, rude, cruel, not to trust;
Enjoyed no sooner but despised straight;
Past reason hunted, and no sooner had,
Past reason hated as a swallowed bait
On purpose laid to make the taker mad;
Mad in pursuit, and in possession so;
Had, having, and in quest to have, extreme;
A bliss in proof, and proved, a very woe,
Before, a joy proposed, behind, a dream.
  All this the world well knows, yet none knows well
  To shun the heaven that leads men to this hell.
                              (*The Sonnets* 129)

Chapter 53 The Heavens More Just

Poor naked wretches, wheresoe'er you are,
That bide the pelting of this pitiless storm,
How shall your houseless heads and unfed sides,
Your looped and windowed raggedness, defend you
From seasons as these? . . . Take physic, pomp;
Expose thyself to feel what wretches feel,
That thou mayst shake the superflux to them,
And show the heavens more just.
                    (*King Lear* 3.4.28-36)

Chapter 54 Virtuous Deeds

> Didst you never hear
> That things ill got had ever bad success?
> And happy always was it for that son
> Whose father for his hoarding went to hell?
> Leave [thy] son [thy] virtuous deeds behind;
> . . .
> For all the rest is held at such a rate
> As brings a thousandfold more care to keep
> Than in possession any jot of pleasure.
> *(3 Henry VI* 2.2.45-53)

> Virtue is bold, and goodness never fearful.
> *(Measure for Measure* 3.1.208)

Chapter 55 When You Do Dance

> When you do dance, I wish you
> A wave o' th' sea, that you might ever do
> Nothing but that – move still, still so,
> And own no other function. Each your doing,
> So singular in each particular,
> Crowns what you are doing in the present deeds,
> That all your acts are queens.
> *(The Winter's Tale* 4.4.140-146)

Chapter 56 A Good Divine

If to do were as easy as to know what were good
to do, chapels had been churches, and poor men's
cottages princes' palaces. It is a good divine that
follows his own instructions; I can easier teach
twenty what were good to be done than to be one
of the twenty to follow mine own teaching.
            (*The Merchant of Venice* 1.2.12-17)

Do not, as some ungracious pastors do,
Show me the steep and thorny way to heaven,
Whiles, like a puffed and reckless libertine,
Himself the primrose path of dalliance treads,
And recks not his own rede. (*Hamlet* 1.3.47-51)

They should be good men, their affairs as righteous;
But all hoods make not monks. (*Henry VIII* 3.1.22-23)

Chapter 57 Proud Man

            Man, proud man,
Dressed in a little brief authority,
Most ignorant of what he's most assured,
His glassy essence, like an angry ape,
Plays such fantastic tricks before high heaven
As makes the angels weep.
      (*Measure for Measure* 2.2.118-123)

He that is proud eats up himself. Pride

is his own glass, his own trumpet, his own chronicle;
and whatever praise itself but in the deed, devours the
deed in the praise. (*Troilus and Cressida* 2.3.154-157)

Chapter 58 Grief Joys, Joy Grieves.

Purpose is but the slave to memory,
Of violent birth, but poor validity,
Which now like fruit unripe sticks on the tree,
But fall unshaken when they mellow be.
Most necessary 'tis that we forget
To pay ourselves what to ourselves is debt.
What to ourselves in passion we propose,
The passion ending, doth the purpose lose.
The violence of either grief or joy
Their own enactures with themselves destroy:
Where joy most revels, grief doth most lament;
Grief joys, joy grieves, on slender accident.
                    (*Hamlet* 3.2.192-203)

Chapter 59 The Web of Our Life

The web of our life is of a mingled yarn,
good and ill together; our virtues would be proud if
our faults whipped them not, and our crimes would
despair if they were not cherished by our virtues.
            (*All's Well That Ends Well* 4.1.71-74)

Chapter 60 From Lowest Place

Strange is it that our bloods,
Of color, weight, and heat, poured all together,
Would quite confound distinction, yet stands off
In differences so mighty. . . .
From lowest place when virtuous things proceed,
The place is dignified by th' doer's deed.
Where great additions swell's and virtue none,
It is a dropsied honor. Good alone
Is good, without a name; vileness is so:
The property by what it is should go,
Not by the title. (*All's Well That Ends Well* 2.3.119-132)

Chapter 61 The Harmony of Peace

A peace is of the nature of a conquest,
For then both parties nobly are subdued.
And neither party loser. (*2 Henry IV* 4.2.89-91)

"My peace we will begin. . . .
Although the victor, we submit to Caesar
And to the Roman empire, promising
To pay our wonted tribute." . . .
The fingers of the pow'rs above do tune
The harmony of this peace.
                . . . our princely eagle,
Th' imperial Caesar, should again unite
His favor with the radiant Cymbeline,
Which shines here in the west. (*Cymbeline* 5.5.459-476)

Chapter 62 Soul of Goodness in Things Evil

There is some soul of goodness in things evil,
Would men observingly distill it out;
For our bad neighbour makes us early stirrers,
Which is both healthful, and husbandry.
Besides, they are our outward consciences,
And preachers to us all, admonishing
That we should dress us fairly for our end.
Thus may we gather honey from the weed,
And make a moral of the devil himself.
      (*Henry V* 4.1.4-12)

Chapter 63 Mighty Fire

Those that with haste will make a mighty fire
Begin it with weak straws.
     (*Julius Caesar* 1.3.107-108)

Chapter 64 Small Lights

Small lights are soon blown out; huge fires abide
And with the wind in greater fury fret.
     (*The Rape of Lucrece* 647-648)

A little fire is quickly trodden out;
Which, being suffered, rivers cannot quench.
     (*3 Henry VI* 4.8.7-8)

Chapter 65 Ignorant of Ourselves

> We, ignorant of ourselves,
> Beg often our own harms, which the wise pow'rs
> Deny us for our good.
> (*Antony and Cleopatra* 2.1.5-7)

When we are born, we cry that we are come
To this great stage of fools. (*King Lear* 4.6.182-83)

Chapter 66 Princes

Princes are the glass, the school, the book,
Where subjects' eyes do learn, do read, do look.
(*The Rape of Lucrece* 615-16)

> Princes are
> A model which heaven makes like to itself:
> As jewels lose their glory if neglected,
> So princes their renowns if not respected.
> (*Pericles* 2.2.10-13)

Chapter 67 The Best Men

> Love all, trust a few,
> Do wrong to none; be able for thine enemy
> Rather in power than use, and keep thy friend
> Under thy own life's key. Be checked for silence,
> But never taxed for speech.
> (*All's Well That Ends Well* 1.1.57-61)

Men of few words are the best men. (*Henry V* 3.2.37)

Chapter 68 Heat Not a Furnace for Your Foe.

Heat not a furnace for your foe so hot
That it do singe yourself. We may outrun
By violent swiftness that which we run at,
And lose by overrunning. Know you not
The fire that mounts the liquor till't run o'er
In seeming to augment it wastes it?
                (*Henry VIII* 1.1.140-145)

Chapter 69 Captain's Captain

Better to leave undone, than by our deed
Acquire too high a fame when him we serve's away...
Who does i' th' wars more than his captain can
Becomes his captain's captain; and ambition
(The soldier's virtue) rather makes choice of loss
Than gain which darkens him.
                (*Antony and Cleopatra* 3.1.14-24)

Chapter 70 As Your Pearl in Your Foul Oyster.

The fish lives in the sea, and 'tis much pride
For fair without the fair within to hide.
                (*Romeo and Juliet* 1.3.89-90)

Rich honesty dwells like a miser in a poor
house as your pearl in your foul oyster.
>   (*As You Like It* 5.4.58-59)

Chapter 71 Speak Less

Have more than thou showest,
Speak less than thou knowest,
Lend less than thou owest,
Ride more than thou goest,
Learn more than thou trowest,
Set less than thou throwest;
Leave thy drink and thy whore.
>   (*King Lear* 1.4.120-126)

Chapter 72 Universal Wolf

Force should be right, or rather right and wrong -
Between whose endless jar justice resides -
Should lose their names, and so should justice too.
Then everything include itself in power,
Power into will, will into appetite,
And appetite, an universal wolf,
So doubly seconded with will and power,
Must make perforce an universal prey
And last eat up himself.
>   (*Troilus and Cressida* 1.3.116-24)

Chapter 73 Bear Free and Patient Thoughts.

Bear free and patient thoughts. (*King Lear* 4.6.79)

The gnarling sorrow hath less power to bite
The man that mocks at it and sets it light.
       (*Richard II* 1.3.291-292)

To mourn a mischief that is past and gone
Is the next way to draw new mischief on.
What cannot be preserved when fortune takes,
Patience her injury a mock'ry makes.
The robbed that smiles, steals something from the thief;
He robs himsef that spends a bootless grief.
              (*Othello* 1.3.201-206)

When the sea was calm all boats alike
Showed mastership in floating; fortune's blows
When most struck home, being gentle wounded craves
A noble cunning. (*Coriolanus* 4.1.6-9)

Chapter 74 Restful Death

Tired with all these, for restful death I cry,
As, to behold desert a beggar born,
And needy nothing trimmed in jollity,
And purest faith unhappily forsworn,
And gilded honor shamefully misplaced,
And maiden virtue rudely strumpeted,
And right perfection wrongfully disgraced,

And strength by limping sway disabled,
And art made tongue-tied by authority,
And folly (doctorlike) controlling skill,
And simple truth miscalled simplicity,
And captive good attending captain ill.
　Tired with all these, from these would I be gone,
　Save that to die, I leave my love alone.
　　　　　　　　　　(*The Sonnets* 66)

Chapter 75 Poor Rich Gain

Those that much covet are with gain so fond
That what they have not, that which they possess
They scatter and unloose it from their bond,
And so by hoping more they have but less,
Or, gaining more, the profit of excess
Is but to surfeit, and such griefs sustain
That they prove bankrupt in this poor rich gain.
　　　　　　　　(*The Rape of Lucrece* 134-140)

What win I if I gain the thing I seek?
A dream, a breath, a froth of fleeting joy.
Who buys a minute's mirth to wail a week?
Or sells eternity to get a toy?
For one sweet grape who will the vine destroy?
Or what fond beggar, but to touch the crown,
Would with the scepter straight be stroken down?
　　　　　　　　(*The Rape of Lucrece* 211-217)

Chapter 76 Violent Fires

His rash fierce blaze of riot cannot last,
For violent fires soon burn out themselves.
Small showers last long, but sudden storms are short;
He tires betimes that spurs too fast betimes.
(*Richard II* 2.1.33-36)

Chapter 77 Noble Respect

The kinder we, to give them thanks for nothing.
Our sport shall be to take what they mistake:
And what poor duty cannot do, noble respect
Takes it in might, not merit.
    (*A Midsummer Night's Dream* 5.1.89-92)

Use every man after his desert, and who shall
scape whipping? Use them after your own honor
and dignity. The less they deserve, the more
merit is in your bounty. (*Hamlet* 2.2.536-539)

Chapter 78 Virtue and cunning

Virtue and cunning [are] endowments greater
Than nobleness and riches: careless heirs
May the two latter darken and expend,
But immortality attends the former,
Making a man a god. . . .
. . . to be thirsty after tottering honor,

Or tie my treasure up in silken bags,
To please the Fool and Death.
>   (*Pericles* 3.2.27-42)

Chapter 79 The Only Peacemaker

I knew when seven justices could not take up a quarrel,
but when the parties were met themselves, one of them
thought but of an If: as, "If you said so, then I said so";
and they shook hands and swore brothers. Your If is
the only peacemaker. Much virtue in If.
>   (*As You Like It* 5.4.98-103)

Chapter 80 In the Commonwealth

I' th' commonwealth I would by contraries
Execute all things. For no kind of traffic
Would I admit; no name of magistrate;
Letters should not be known; riches, poverty,
And use of service, none; contract, succession,
Bourn, bound of land, tilth, vineyard, none;
No use of metal, corn, or wine, or oil;
No occupation; all men idle, all;
And women too, but innocent and pure;
No sovereignty. . . .
All things in common nature should produce
Without sweat or endeavor. Treason, felony,
Sword, pike, knife, gun, or need of any engine
Would I not have; but nature should bring forth,

Of it own kind, all foison, all abundance,
To feed my innocent people.
> (*The Tempest* 2.1.152-169)

Chapter 81 The More I Give to Thee

It is not enough to speak, but to speak true.
> (*A Midsummer Night's Dream* 5.1.120-121)

Suit the action to the word, the word to the action,
with this special observance, that you o'erstep not
the modesty of nature. (*Hamlet* 3.2.17-9)

Antony: There's beggary in the love that can be reckoned.
Cleopatra: I'll set a bourn how far to be beloved.
Antony: Then must thou needs find out new heaven, new earth.
> (*Antony and Cleopatra* 1.1.15-17)

My bounty is as boundless as the sea,
My love as deep; the more I give to thee,
The more I have. (*Romeo and Juliet* 2.2.134-35)

셰익스피어 정전正典 목록
The Shakespeare Canon

희곡 Plays

1588-93	『실수연발』	(*The Comedy of Errors*)
1588-92	『헨리 6세 2부』	(*2 Henry VI*)
1588-92	『헨리 6세 3부』	(*3 Henry VI*)
1588-92	『헨리 6세 1부』	(*1 Henry VI*)
1592-93	『리처드 3세』	(*Richard III*)
1592-94	『타이터스 앤드로니쿠스』	(*Titus Andronicus*)
1593-94	『말괄량이 길들이기』	(*The Taming of the Shrew*)
1593-94	『베로나의 두 신사』	(*The Two Gentlemen of Verona*)
1588-95	『사랑의 헛수고』	(*Love's Labor's Lost*)
1594-96	『로미오와 줄리엣』	(*Romeo and Juliet*)
1595	『리처드 2세』	(*Richard II*)
1594-96	『한여름 밤의 꿈』	(*A Midsummer Night's Dream*)
1590-97	『존 왕』	(*King John*)
1596-97	『베니스의 상인』	(*The Merchant of Venice*)
1597	『헨리 4세 1부』	(*1 Henry IV*)
1597-98	『헨리 4세 2부』	(*2 Henry IV*)
1598-1600	『헛소동』	(*Much Ado About Nothing*)
1598-99	『헨리 5세』	(*Henry V*)
1599	『줄리어스 시저』	(*Julius Caesar*)
1599-1600	『좋으실 대로』	(*As You Like It*)
1600-02	『십이야』	(*Twelfth Night*)
1600-01	『햄릿』	(*Hamlet*)
1597-1601	『윈저의 즐거운 아낙네들』	(*The Merry Wives of Windsor*)
1601-02	『트로일러스와 크레시다』	(*Troilus and Cressida*)
1602-04	『끝이 좋으면 모두 좋다』	(*All's Well That Ends Well*)
1603-04	『오셀로』	(*Othello*)

1604	『자에는 자로』 (*Measure for Measure*)
1604-09	『아테네의 타이몬』 (*Timon of Athens*)
1605-06	『리어 왕』 (*King Lear*)
1605-06	『맥베스』 (*Macbeth*)
1606-07	『안토니와 클레오파트라』 (*Antony and Cleopatra*)
1607-09	『코리오레이너스』 (*Coriolanus*)
1608-09	『페리클레스』 (*Pericles*)
1609-10	『심벨린』 (*Cymbeline*)
1610-11	『겨울 이야기』 (*The Winter's Tale*)
1611	『태풍』 (*The Tempest*)
1612-13	『헨리 8세』 (*Henry VIII*)
1613	『두 귀족 친척』 (*The Two Noble Kinsmen*)

시 Poems

1592	『비너스와 아도니스』 (*Venus and Adonis*)
1533-94	『루크리스의 능욕』 (*The Rape of Lucrece*)
1593-1600	『소네트』 (*The Sonnets*)

윌리엄 셰익스피어 연표

1564년	잉글랜드 워릭셔주 남부에 위치한 스트랫퍼드어폰에이번 Stratford-upon-Avon에서 아버지 존 셰익스피어John Shakespeare와 어머니 메리 아든Mary Arden 사이의 맏아들로 출생 (4월 23일)
1565년	존 셰익스피어, 참사의원alderman으로 선출
1568년	존 셰익스피어, 스트랫퍼드의 최고 행정관bailiff으로 선출됨
1582년	윌리엄 셰익스피어, 여덟 살 위의 앤 해서웨이Anne Hathaway와 결혼
1583년	맏딸 수잔나Susanna 출생
1585년	쌍둥이 햄넷Hamnet과 주디스Judith 출생
1588년	스페인의 무적함대Armada가 영국 해군에게 패함 (7월 28일)
1594년	궁내 장관 극단의 단원이 됨
1596년	아들 햄넷(11살)이 알 수 없는 원인으로 사망
1597년	고향 스트랫퍼드에서 둘째로 큰 저택 뉴플레이스New Place 저택 구입
1599년	템스 강 남쪽에 글로브 극장Globe Theatre 건립 글로브 극장 공동 경영인이 됨
1601년	부친 존 셰익스피어 사망
1603년	엘리자베스 여왕 사망. 제임스 1세 즉위
1607년	맏딸 수잔나가 스트랫퍼드의 의사 존 홀John Hall과 결혼 동생 에드먼드 런던에서 사망
1608년	셰익스피어의 모친 메리 사망. 수잔나의 맏딸 엘리자베스 출생
1610년	고향 스트랫퍼드로 귀향
1611년	흠정영역欽定英譯성서 *King James Bible* 출판
1613년	사극 『헨리 8세』 공연 중 글로브 극장 화재로 소실. 동생 리처드 사망
1616년	둘째 딸 주디스가 토머스 퀴니Thomas Quiney와 결혼 (2월 20일) 윌리엄 셰익스피어 고향 스트랫퍼드에서 52세로 사망 (4월 23일)
1623년	셰익스피어 부인 앤 셰익스피어 사망 (8월 8일) 존 헤밍John Heminges과 헨리 컨들Henry Condell이 셰익스피어 첫 번째 2절판(First Folio) 전집 출간